Professional Development Management
Series Editor: Dr Harry Tolley

Developing
as a
Teacher of
Geography

Tony Fisher

University of Nottingham

D1344517

Chris Kington Publishing
CAMBRIDGE

© Tony Fisher
1998

ISBN 1 899857 17 6

First published 1998 by
Chris Kington Publishing
27 Rathmore Road
Cambridge CB1 4AB

British Library cataloguing in publication data. A catalogue record for this book is available from the British Library.

Printed in the United Kingdom by York Publishing Services Ltd, 64 Hallfield Road, Layerthorpe, York Y03 7XQ

Contents

Author's preface

In any book which attempts to cover the teaching of geography in under 100 pages there will be a trade-off between coverage and depth. I have attempted to resolve this by going into more depth about those aspects of the teaching of geography which seem to me to warrant attention through being any or all of: important; interesting; recent and/or topical; not much covered elsewhere.

Other things are mentioned very much as 'start points' for the intellectual enquiry of the new teacher, who will look to practice and to other writers in developing their own ideas and approaches. Also, I have tried to put a particular 'spin' on the aspects of teaching and learning in geography included here - rather than stick to a traditionally subject-centred perspective I have attempted to explicitly address the professional development of the student teacher/newly qualified/recently qualified teacher who has some geography to teach. To any of these users, I hope you find this book useful and stimulating.

Jazz musicians speak of 'payin' dues'. Here are mine as writer of this book. My partner, Joyce Oldfield, and my immediate colleague, Mary Biddulph, gave great support including helping me find the space at work and at home to write the book under considerable pressure of time. Joyce also did the proof-reading and some valuable 'critical friending'. I have no secretary to thank for transforming my indecipherable manuscript (because there was no indecipherable manuscript in that sense) - just my trusty Acorn RISC PC. Harry Tolley, the series editor, has been a source of advice and enthusiasm over a number of years; his confidence in me has provided both support and challenge. A true mentor.

To acknowledge what one has gained from one's colleagues and students over the years may be a cliché, but is no less true for that, so to more people associated with Rushcliffe School, West Bridgford, the Nottinghamshire Education Support Service as was (and in particular the then National Curriculum Support Team) and the School of Education at the University of Nottingham than I can name, thanks.

Tony Fisher

March 1998

Introduction

Geography in schools appears in several guises. In England and Wales it is a statutory requirement in the National Curriculum for the age range 5 to 14, and optional beyond that in the form of various examination syllabi. Sometimes it bears its own label. Sometimes it is merged in with one or more other aspects of the curriculum. But, whichever its guise in any particular school, age group or curricular framework, it falls to some teachers to plan, teach and evaluate it.

This book is aimed in particular at those who are in the early stages of becoming teachers, (and teaching is perhaps most accurately conceived as a constant state of 'becoming') whose work will involve some geography. This therefore includes:

- *student teachers;*
- *newly qualified teachers (NQTs);*
- *recently qualified teachers (RQTs).*

In terms of geography, the book is aimed at:

- *teachers of geography as a separate 'subject' (normally in the secondary age range);*
- *teachers of a range of subjects of which geography may be just one part, ie*
    - *primary school teachers,*
    - *teachers of humanities or other interdisciplinary courses in the secondary school.*

But this is not a book about geography as a subject, nor indeed simply a book about geography teaching per se. Rather, it is a book which attempts to address the professional development of those who will teach geography. This does not mean there is nothing about the teaching of geography in the book - far from it! But it does represent a slightly different emphasis. The focus of the book is on you, the individual teacher in the early stages of your career, and on the processes of professional development which can, perhaps should, characterise this phase, rather than simply on the business of 'geography-and-how-to-teach-it', which tends to emphasise the subject whilst leaving your individual professional development implicit. As such this book complements the **Beginning Teaching Workbooks** series and the **Professional Development Management File**, with which it is closely related.

The basic thesis here is that the professional development which takes place in the early years of a teaching career is of fundamental importance, and that the beginner teacher who can function as a self-developing, autonomous professional will be best placed to gain the maximum benefit from these processes. Such an individual will, as a consequence, be able to maximise her/his contribution to the whole purpose of providing quality teaching and learning for young people - and in the case of this book that will be in the subject area we know as 'geography'.

A note about autonomy, individualism and collaboration

In the preceding comments I have stressed the idea of your developing a degree of 'professional autonomy'. By this I mean having a sense of your own professional development, and a level of personal empowerment to enable you to act independently when appropriate or necessary. This, as we shall see, includes the capability to carry out rigorous self-evaluation. In practice your level of professional autonomy as a teacher of geography (and other aspects of the curriculum) will normally increase as you develop your pedagogic knowledge, skills and understandings, and as a consequence your confidence.

This notion of autonomy is of course compatible with another aspect of your development as a teacher which this book, and others in the **Beginning Teaching Workbooks** series, can also be seen to stress - that of collaboration. Collaboration is important as it is the means by which you as a developing teacher become part of the community of the school in which you work, and of the wider professional community. Also, it is the means by which the 'you-as-teacher' emerges, through negotiation and professional discourse. But you can only participate meaningfully in such negotiation and discourse if you have autonomy. "...In a very real sense, teachers cannot be empowered, they can only empower, or choose, themselves... 'Power is never given; it's taken'." (Bullough et al, 1991, p.193)

You probably will have recognised that this notion of the self-empowering, autonomous, collaborative teacher is not at all the same thing as the 'individualist'. Individualism here is taken to

*Many of the ideas described in this section are developed in more detail in **Emerging as a Teacher**, Chapter 10, Teacher Education and Teacher Development. (Bullough et al, 1991)*

mean the opposite of the collaborative, community-oriented approach. In its rejection of collaborative approaches, individualism deprives the individual of the benefits of sharing in communal processes, and deprives the community of the benefit of that individual's participation. It denies the communal basis of the process of education.

Of course autonomy and collaboration, or indeed individualism, can be fostered given a particular set of prevailing circumstances and values in a given school. But you have a role to play and choices to make too.

The aims of this book

Reading this book will not *make* you a better teacher! However, it is certainly the aim that this book will *support* you in becoming a better teacher. The overall aim therefore is to provide guidance which will support you in becoming:

- *autonomous and self-reliant;*
- *pro-active in the face of changing circumstances;*
- *self-developing as a reflective practitioner;*
- *committed to continuous improvement;*
- *a collaborative member of varying scales of professional community, through the development of your teaching of geography.*

Your professional autonomy as a developing teacher of geography will reflect:

- *your achievement of professional competence;*
- *your ability to conduct meaningful action research aimed at improving classroom practice;*
- *your ability to think critically about aspects of education;*
- *your personal sense of empowerment;*
- *your 'ownership' of your own professional development.*

The underlying premise is that the educational world, which has seen significant change over recent years, will continue to change in ways which are not always predictable. This is true both of education in general, and of the subject of geography in particular. Your 'teaching professionalism' will therefore reflect your ability to function purposefully in the midst of uncertainty, to articulate and take account of underlying educational values yet to be flexible in coping with change. As such a teacher you will have a clear idea through self-review of your own development needs. You will also develop a 'portfolio' of skills, knowledge and understandings to enable you both to seek and to respond to a range of opportunities.

Achieving the aims

In order to achieve the aims identified above, the focus of this book will be on developing the underlying teaching competences in the context of the teaching of geography. To maximise the potential for addressing your professional development the approach will be permeated by a number of the key processes from the **Beginning Teaching Workbooks**, which are:

- *self activation and 'taking responsibility';*
- *structured classroom observation;*
- *using learning partnerships;*
- *action research;*
- *discussion;*
- *reading;*
- *reflection;*
- *action planning;*
- *log or journal-keeping;*
- *development of competences.*

By its nature the book will have to some extent a modular rather than a strictly sequential structure. You will chart your own course through some parts of it reflecting your own particular needs and circumstances. The underlying structure of this book is summarised in **Figure 1**, below.

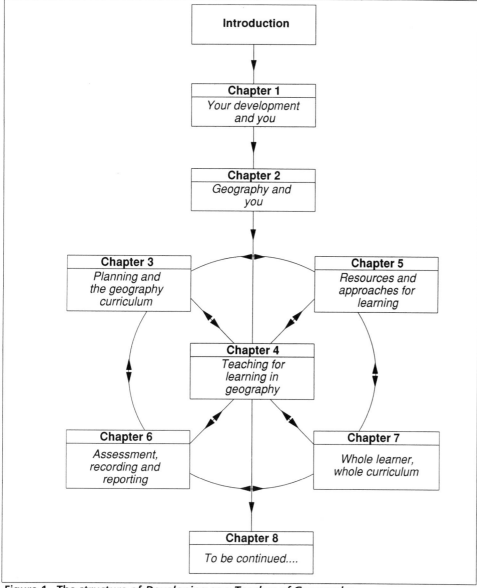

Because of the links between this book and the Beginning Teaching Workbooks series you may well find it helpful to use this book in conjunction with relevant books from the series; some links are identified in the text and in the margin notes.

Figure 1   The structure of *Developing as a Teacher of Geography*

After this introduction come two Chapters which you are strongly recommended to work through before using the other Chapters in the more flexible manner referred to above.

Chapter 1: Your development and you looks at the development of competences, action research and reflection as essential underpinnings of your development as a teacher of geography.

Chapter 2: Geography and you follows on by making explicit the connection between your professional development and the subject of geography and by looking briefly at the development of geography itself.

Having used these two Chapters to 'prepare the ground', you will be in a position to make best use of Chapters 3 to 7. It is envisaged that you will use these in a more flexible way as appropriate to your individual needs and circumstances. Each Chapter addresses a major area of competence.

Chapter 3: Planning and the geography curriculum looks at the planning process at a range of scales, including the individual lesson. It emphasises the relationship between individual planning and external requirements, such as the National Curriculum, and focuses on planning for an enquiry approach.

Chapter 4: Teaching for learning in geography presents a holistic view of teaching and learning as interconnected, complementary activities, and focuses on the learning outcomes and aspects of differentiation.

Chapter 5: Resources and approaches for learning takes a broadly defined perspective on resources before looking specifically at the following approaches to teaching and learning in geography: the development of a sense of place; fieldwork; the use of information technology (IT); active learning; the development of graphicacy.

Chapter 6: Assessment, recording and reporting considers these generic aspects of teaching as they relate to the teaching of geography.

Chapter 7: Whole learner, whole curriculum examines the relationship between geography and aspects of the 'whole curriculum' in the context of an understanding of educational ideologies. It pays particular attention to the relationship between geography and language development, and the development of thinking skills.

Chapter 8: To be continued... focuses on two aspects of the future: teaching about the future and your on-going professional development. It concludes with two contrasting self-review activities.

The activities: getting the most from this book

In Beginning Teaching Workbook 2: Beginning Initial Teacher Training (Tolley et al, 1996) we identified the desirability of working with a **peer partner**. The desirability of this is not restricted to student teachers. Such a person is one in a similar situation and of a similar stage of development to yourself, and with whom you feel comfortable collaborating and having the type of discussion referred to here.

When a peer partnership works well it can soon develop into a **'learning partnership'** and then into a relationship in which you are each a **'critical friend'** for the other in a trusting, open, supportively critical relationship.

If you do not yet have a peer partner, you are strongly advised to seek one now.

All Chapters in this book contain suggested activities. The activities provide contexts for you to make links between your own experience and circumstances in teaching, and the ideas contained in this book and the other sources to which it refers. Some of the activities are of a type which can be done relatively quickly, perhaps through reflection and without making special arrangements. Others are more in the nature of small action research projects which by their nature take place over a longer time-span, perhaps involving careful planning, negotiation and data collection.

You will have to judge which of the activities are appropriate to your needs and situation at a given time. These decisions could be taken either in consultation with someone with responsibility for the oversight of your professional development (eg your tutor, mentor, professional tutor, head of department or team leader), or with someone in a similar position to yourself - a **peer partner**. Indeed, some of the activities are designed with a collaborative approach with a peer partner in mind.

It is unlikely that you will do all of the activities in this book, but they are far from being an optional extra. There is a basic assumption here that teaching is all about learning, in this case your own professional learning, and the activities are designed to promote that learning. If you do not do most of the activities, you will not get the most from this book.

1

Your development and you

"Discourses of competence attempt to repress certain conceptions of knowledge and understanding in order to sustain an agenda where competence-based qualifications appear to be the appropriate response. A regime of truth is established which derides certain forms of knowledge as 'theory', irrelevant to 'getting the job done well'."

Usher and Edwards, 1994, p. 115

Aims

This Chapter focuses on you and the things you can do to take ownership of your professional development. In particular it sets out to look at the following aspects of your development:

- *competence development and monitoring;*
- *action research;*
- *reflection.*

I hope to achieve a balance similar to that described by my earlier use of the phrase 'self-empowering, autonomous, collaborative teacher', and in so doing begin to address the concern voiced by Usher and Edwards which begins this Chapter. They articulate a view which many have about the limitations of competence-based approaches to teacher education, coupling (rightly) the rise of such approaches with an attack on 'theory'. They go on to say that:

"... the competent teacher is constructed not as one who knows that something is the case, or knows how to teach, but who can actually teach competently according to pre-determined criteria of competences. The veiling of certain forms of knowledge as 'theory' to be removed from the curricula of teacher training is something which also finds support among many trainee teachers, who thereby deny themselves the forms of autonomy and the right to be critical which were previously the defining characteristics of the teaching profession."

This appears to leave competences and theory set in opposition to each other, as if they are necessarily incompatible. Usher and Edwards may indeed be right in their radical critique of the 'competence movement' and what it signifies about the way in which work-related aspects of society are constructed and power relations manitained, but for the time being at least, specified competences are a non-negotiable aspect of becoming a teacher. Is the professionally competent, yet critically reflective, theorising, autonomous teacher too much to hope for?

A note on spellings
In this book I have used 'competence' as the singular form and 'competences' as the plural form. I have avoided therefore the use of the term 'competency' and its plural form, 'competencies'.

Standards, competence development and monitoring

Lists of competences against which new entrants to the profession could be judged were issued by the then Council for the Accreditation of Teacher Education (CATE) in 1992 for secondary school teachers, and in 1993 for primary school teachers. These competences were criticised by many (including the author) for being too narrow, prescriptive, incomplete, reductive, atomising and so on. They have now been replaced by the *Standards for the Award of Qualified Teacher Status* (TTA, 1997), a not dissimilar, if more detailed, list. Though now referred to by the Teacher Training Agency (TTA) as 'standards' rather than 'competences', "the standards have been written to be specific, explicit and assessable" (TTA, p.2), and are thus still statements of competence. They define the 'essential core' of teaching capability for those who seek to qualify as teachers.

There is also a case for continuing to use competences as a basis for reflection and self-review beyond the award of qualified teacher status (QTS), because they can be a helpful means of focusing on aspects of teaching. In doing so we must not, of course, lose sight of one of the most important - though frequently unstated or overlooked - aspect of the competences: that of the need for synergy *between* them. A mere assemblage of competences does not make a teacher: the whole is greater than the sum of the parts. (See also margin note)

Having touched on some notes of caution around the use of competences we now need to consider what part they may play in your professional development as a teacher. Most lists of

In the Introduction to **Standards for the Award of Qualified Teacher Status** *(TTA, 1992) the TTA warn that though the standards are set out "discretely", "professionalism... implies more than meeting a series of discrete standards. It is necessary to consider the standards as a whole to appreciate the creativity, commitment, energy and enthusiasm which teaching demands, and the intellectual and managerial skills required of the effective professional." (p.2)*

competences are stated in a generic, rather than subject-specific way. You should interpret the generic statements in the light of your circumstances.

Activity

1. Find out which list of competences/standards is being used in your development as a teacher. Make sure you have your own copy of the list, and that you understand it fully.
2. Examine the list to identify those statements where your knowledge and understanding of geography will be required (both explicitly and implicitly).
3. Begin to keep a folder or file containing your personal record of professional development, including the relevant list of competences.

Action research

> "... action research provides a method for testing and improving educational practices, and basing the practices and procedures of teaching on theoretical knowledge and research organised by professional teachers."
>
> *Carr and Kemmis, 1986, p. 221*

In essence the action research approach involves making a small-scale, deliberate intervention in an aspect of the area of interest - in this case education (and, specifically, the teaching of geography) - and careful study of the consequences. Though it can be undertaken by an individual teacher, it is often undertaken collaboratively by a group actively involved in the area of interest: thus it is both research *in* action and research *into* action. An action research cycle is normally made up of four stages: planning, action, observation and reflection (Hillcoat, 1996, p.151). As such it has similarities with Kolb's model of experiential learning, as shown in **Figure 1.1.**

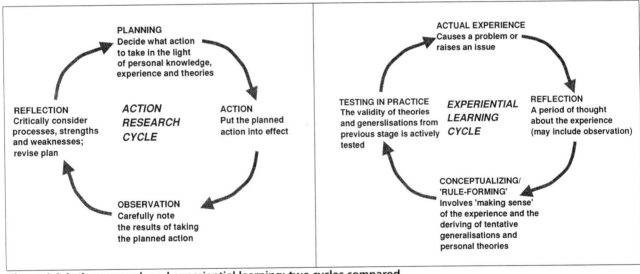

Figure 1.1 Action research and experiential learning: two cycles compared

Action research goes hand-in-hand with the development of teaching to become a genuinely professional activity (Carr and Kemmis). So, as a teacher of geography (amongst other things), you will want to use action research to investigate and develop aspects of your work.

It may well be that, if you are reading this at an early stage in your preparation to become a teacher, you are not yet in a position to carry out action research *per se*. However, you are almost certainly in a situation where there are some things which you need to find out through investigation (which at this stage may be as simple as asking the appropriate person the right question). Possibilities for action research will be indicated in the later sections of this book, and will be based on an assumption that you will be approaching your work in a questioning, investigative manner. Implicit in this is the further assumption that, because you are approaching your work in such a manner, you will identify your own opportunities for investigation and requirements for information and insights. Note them. Act on them!

As we shall see, there are also similarities between the **investigative** *approach towards the development of practice, which you are being encouraged to adopt here, and the* **enquiry** *approach to learning in geography which will become an important aspect of your geographical methodology.*

Activity

1. Investigate the position of geography in the curriculum of the school where you are placed. You may wish to be guided by the following questions:
    *   Who is in charge of geography in the school?
    *   Who teaches geography?
    *   How much time is given to geography?
    *   How does geography appear, eg separate subject, topic component, interdisciplinary course?
    *   Do all youngsters in the school experience a similar 'entitlement' to geography?
    *   Is there a written policy or statement for geography, or a set of aims and objectives?

Reflection

"There is nothing either good or bad, but thinking makes it so."

Hamlet, II ii

"The tendency to judge - to dichotomise good and bad, success and failure - seems to be strongest when the complexity of our circumstances outstrips our ability to understand them."

Holly, 1987, p. 7

Reflection is here taken to mean 'a thoughtful and searching deliberation' on some aspect of knowledge or experience. Such reflection is thus not merely a reliving of the experience or a rehearsal of the knowledge. To be of value to your developing professionalism as a teacher, your reflection will be guided and shaped by a sense of purpose which will itself embody at least some of the following objectives:

*   *to clarify what has happened or what is known;*
*   *to examine what is known or experienced, from a range of perspectives;*
*   *to question underlying assumptions;*
*   *to tease out new insights and develop new understandings;*
*   *to formulate new questions;*
*   *to lead to improvements in practice.*

Teacher reflection was identified by Schön (1987) as a key process in learning to teach and a vital source of teachers' professional knowledge. Schön identifies three types of cognitive process which are helpful in understanding the role of reflection:

*   *knowing-in-action;*
*   *reflection-in-action;*
*   *reflection-on-action.*

Knowing-in-action is the 'intelligent action' which competent teachers display through what they do in a given set of circumstances. Such competence is not easily articulated in response to questions such as "Why and how did you do that?" This is because the action is effectively intuitive, so deeply embedded is the knowledge. No conscious reflective thought is involved.

Reflection-in-action is a natural, sometimes unbidden response to a new situation, eg "Hmmm... Now why doesn't Ben understand my explanation of erosion? What if I try it this way?" This is likely to take place during the teaching activity, at a conscious level, and is therefore referred to by Schön as 'reflection-in-action'.

Reflection-on-action is more deliberate, taking place through the articulation and examination of something after it is over. It is a conscious, probing re-examination of events, guided by the objectives listed above. Reflection-on-action seeks to yield the kinds of insights and professional knowledge which will support improvements in practice and increased professional autonomy. It is a necessary condition for worthwhile action research to take place, and a vital component of the action research cycle. For you, reflection-on-action is a vital part of your professional learning as it brings to a conscious level the knowledge which guides your actions and subjects it to scrutiny. It is the means by which you gain control over the you-as-teacher.

A simple analogy

You are driving your car. A child runs out into the road. You perform an emergency stop. This is 'knowing-in-action'. You know how to stop the car without thinking (though in this case you could of course say how and why!)

You continue your journey. You meet increasing levels of traffic. You decide to go a different way to see if you can avoid the congestion. This is 'reflection-in-action', because you have thought of and tried out a different course of action whilst en route.

You have arrived at your destination. You think back over the journey, and decide it was too stressful. You are also becoming increasingly concerned about environmental aspects of car usage. You decide to use the train next time. This is 'reflection-on-action', because you are thinking critically about the activity after it is concluded.

But reflection is not just a matter of sitting and thinking. It is important to put into language (spoken or written), descriptions and explanations of aspects of the teaching situation which have been experienced. For this reason you are recommended to keep a **reflective journal** of your experiences in teaching. This is not the same thing as a log which simply records events which happen. It is a 'reconstruction of experience' (Holly, p. 6) with a conscious juxtaposition of objective and subjective dimensions of experience. You can't possibly hope to record everything, so don't even try! Be selective: write about that which interests you. Through the medium of such a journal it is possible for you to conduct a dialogue with your own experience and to examine the development of the professional knowledge which guides your actions as a teacher.

> "*Our teaching becomes not 'good' or 'bad' but part of an ongoing process in a context of interacting elements, some of which are beyond our control and some that are within it. We know more about our classrooms and our teaching than anyone else does, and through reflective writing and collegial discussion, we have many opportunities to be architects of our own improvement.*"
>
> *Holly, p.42*

Activity

Note: You will find as you use the next Chapter ('Geography and you') that there is a natural link back to this activity from the first activity in that Chapter.

1. The activity which concluded the previous section of this Chapter will have provided you with some factual information about geography in the school where you are currently placed. But not all of this will be 'neutral' information. Some of it will have elicited a response from you. Think about these questions:
   - What have you learned about geography in your school?
   - How do you feel about what you have learned about geography in your school?
   - How easy was it to acquire the information?
   - How did you feel whilst getting the information?
   - What impression do you gain from the information and from the process of acquiring it?
   - Are there other questions you would like to ask?
2. On the basis of your answers write an entry in your reflective journal.

Reading and reflection

Reflection on action has as its main focus your experiences in the classroom. Reading can also provide food for thought, either in its own right or as an additional perspective on your classroom experiences. Teaching is, however, a demanding and time-consuming activity, so even if you have time for 'academic' reading, you may not feel much like doing it. The day-to-day job of teaching can demand a lot of reading in its own right, of course. This everyday reading includes:

- *written work for marking;*
- *textbooks and other learning resources for preparation;*
- *new learning materials for evaluation;*
- *letters to and from parents;*
- *memoranda and other printed information circulated in the school;*
- *school, local authority and government policy documents and guidelines.*

The result of this is that some teachers read little from the 'educational literature' once they have qualified, unless they need to find out something for a specific purpose, or decide to study for a higher degree. This move, for some at least, away from reading the educational literature, may also contribute towards the perception of a gap between 'theory' and practice.

To retain 'the reading habit' you may find it supportive to have a reading partner, eg your peer partner. You should agree a realistic target - say a chapter or an article per half term, plus a half hour discussion of the item read, perhaps over lunch. You then need a means of agreeing what it is you will both read - preferably something of current mutual interest.

Action point

Start this arrangement now, perhaps by reading and discussing something chosen from *A Case for Geography* (Bailey and Binns, 1987) in association with working through the next Chapter of this book. Keep a note of your reading, eg in your reflective journal.

2
Geography and you

*"The art of Biography
Is different from Geography.
Geography is about maps,
But Biography is about chaps."*

Edmund Clerihew Bentley

Aims

What is geography to you? A bit more than just 'about maps', it is to be hoped! This Chapter seeks to establish something of the nature of geography. But do not skip it if you already have a geography degree or think you know what geography is! In this Chapter we shall try not only to explore the nature of geography, but to examine where you stand in relation to this. This is vital, as it is the basis from which you will interpret the rest of the book, and the basis from which you will approach the planning, teaching and evaluation of geography in your work. This is equally the case if you are contemplating teaching an A Level geography group, or working with a reception class. It is important to know 'where you're coming from' (to coin a geographical phrase!) because in terms of your development as one who teaches geography, you will inevitably start from where you are.

Your experiences of 'geography'

During your own education you will have had some experiences which will have shaped your personal view of geography and how (or how not) to teach it. It is important to recognise this, because there is no one, single geography 'out there' which you will approach in a neutral way and simply teach.

Firstly, two linked issues - the nature of geography, and how to 'do' it - are, as we shall see, dynamic, problematic and contested. You will be faced with decisions and choices. Secondly, whichever aspects of geography fall to you to teach, be they a National Curriculum Programme of Study, an examination syllabus or a lesson planned by a colleague who is absent, you can only make sense of them in terms of your previous experience. This experience will have provided you with a set of 'constructs', or mental frameworks, which enable you to act and react (decide, plan, teach, evaluate) in circumstances yet to occur, (and in the process create new constructs to guide you further.) Thus that which has yet to happen is inextricably linked via the fleeting present to past experience. And that experience is unique and personal to you.

Activity

"'Where shall I begin, please your Majesty?' he asked.

'Begin at the beginning,' the King said gravely, 'and go on till you come to the end: then stop.'"

Lewis Carroll, 'Alice in Wonderland'

This activity is an adaptation of the process of 'lifemapping' (Kompf, 1995). It can be thought of as a personal audit of remembered experiences with, in this case, a particular focus on geography. It is in the nature of this activity that some of the things you remember will 'unlock' other memories. You may therefore find that you will not complete this activity in one go - indeed, that is unlikely. Nor is it a problem. This activity is on-going in nature.

The purpose of this activity is to provide a clear basis from which you will go on to use this book; not because the geography you have experienced should automatically become the geography you will teach, but because your view of geography will inevitably *influence* the geography you teach and, importantly, *how* you go about it. And these fundamental views are inescapably a product of the experiences you have had.

The process of lifemapping, on which this activity is based, was developed by Michael Kompf. He describes the process fully in a paper Anticipation and Reflection: Non-Prophet Activities? (1995)
(Interestingly, Kompf refers to the process as one of 'lifemapping' and to significant events as being 'landmarks', both terms with a strong geographical resonance.)

Stage one

1. Think back over your own learning, from as far back as you can remember. Try to identify aspects of what you now think of as learning in geography, regardless of whether or not it was called geography at the time.

2. Make a first draft of a chronolgy of your learning in geography on a copy of **Figure 2.1**. Try to allocate specific events or experiences of 'geography' to the chronology, identifying them by a keyword or phrase. Leave spaces or make several drafts, as the recollection of some experiences and events will probably trigger the recall of others.

3. Score each experience in terms of its impact (beneficial / adverse) on you and your view of geography, on a scale of +10 to -10.

4. Is it possible to attach other people to any of the events or experiences because they play a prominent part in how you remember those experiences? Note them and their role (eg teacher).

5. Review the chronology. Is it all school-based? If it is, are there other non-school experiences which you want to add?

Personal chronology of learning in geography					
Year	Age	Event keyword	Impact then (+/- 10)	Others involved	Role

Figure 2.1 Framework for constructing a personal chronology of learning in geography

Stage two

1. Explore the events and experiences listed in stage one more fully, by expanding the keyword into a fuller description of the event or experience.
2. From this fuller description it is important now to extract the meaning and implications each event has for you *at present*. You may want to do this privately on separate sheets of paper, or you may want to do it through discussion with your peer partner.

What will have been achieved through the above process is that the 'geographical you', insofar as you currently identify it, has been brought to the surface. You should now be much clearer about 'where you're coming from' in terms of geographical education. Your reflection on the geography you have experienced, will have enabled you to understand better the teacher of geography you expect to be, now and in the furture. Indeed, you already have your own personal theories about geography and how to teach it.

Geography as others see it

We have already established that your teaching of geography will be influenced by how you see it as a subject, and that this is, in turn, influenced by the experiences you have had. These experiences have shown the imprint of how others see geography. It is to such other views of geography that we now turn our attention.

A working definition of what school geography currently is, at least in the eyes of the Geography National Curriculum Working Group, can be taken from their Final Report:

"*Geography explores the relationship between the Earth and its peoples through the study of place, space and environment. Geographers ask the questions where and what; also how and why.*"

DES, 1990

Activity

1. Critically evaluate the above definition of geography.
2. Does it match your own view of geography? Does what you think of as geography fall within this definition, or are there aspects which would be excluded?
3. Is it important or worthwhile to have such a definition? Is it indeed 'definitive', or does it raise further questions?
4. Who, if anyone, benefits from the existence and nature of such a definition?

Geography's story (one version)

The study of Earth as the home of humankind is the very stuff of geography, under the above definition. But of course how academic geographers, and their schoolteacher counterparts, have seen their task and gone about such study, has altered as the subject has developed. This has not been without argument and controversy, and it is no accident that David Livingstone's authoritative account of the development of the subject - *The Geographical Tradition* - is subtitled 'Episodes in the History of a Contested Enterprise'!

So, geography has changed - is changing. In order to engage as an autonomous participant in curriculum debate about geography (or anything else for that matter), it is important to know something of how others see it, and for that it is necessary to know something of its development.

The earliest geographers were explorers keen to extend the 'known world' and in so doing move from myths to maps (Livingstone, 1992). Subsequently this developed into the constructing of inventories and classifications of phenomena: the 'capes and bays' approach to knowledge about the world (the 'what' and the 'where'). Later, knowledge was to be organised around a regional framework (sometimes 'natural regions', but also countries) as a basis for storing and accessing the by now extensive information about the world. The individuality of places was stressed through sample studies.

This regional case study approach is still something of a stereotype of school geography. This has persisted despite the regional approach being rejected, or at least down-played, by many geographers (and, later, teachers of geography) as the 'quantitative revolution' with its strong positivist basis took hold in the 1960s. The case study approach was seen as somewhat idiosyncratic and unscientific. The regional approach, it was felt, was too deterministic in suggesting, or at least implying, that the nature and distribution of human activity was determined by that of natural phenomena.

No sooner had geography adopted the new 'spatial science' paradigm, with its emphasis on pattern, hypothesis-testing and generalisable theories, than this too came under attack from those who felt that human experience and questions of social justice were being neglected. Under their diverse influence geography became both more humanistic and more radical, going beyond the 'how and why' of theory and explanation to questions of identity ('who?') and value judgement such as 'how ought'.

Against this background four Schools Council projects looked afresh at change in the subject in the 1970s. All took an approach that considered the needs of learners as well as the nature of the subject, and explicitly tackled the issue of values alongside the apparent precision of quanitification. They promoted "a more balanced, eclectic and pluralist approach" to geography in schools. (Marsden, 1995, p. 40)

The Schools Council projects referred to are:
- *Geography for the Young School Leaver (GYSL - The Avery Hill Project),*
- *Geography 14 to 18 (The Bristol Project),*
- *History, Geography and Social Science 8 to 13 (Space, Time and Society),*
- *Geography 16 - 19.*

(For more detail see Marsden, 1995, p. 40 and Derricott in Marsden and Hughes 1994, Chapter 2)

These projects were significant in their impact on school geography, not only because they addressed the questions of geography's place and contribution to the curriculum, but also, importantly, because of their empowerment of teachers as curriculum developers.

Additionally, in some schools teachers of geography were experimenting with links with other subjects and blurring its boundaries in the process. We began to see Humanities and World Studies projects and courses, sometimes influenced by a critical social science perspective. These to some degree paralleled topic-based approaches adopted in many primary schools, particularly in the wake of the Plowden Report and the interpretation given to the Report's principle of child-centredness.

In some primary schools geography was taught from a position of weakness and practice was found by HMI to be unsatisfactory in a majority of schools (DES, 1989). Interestingly, however, and despite the detractors of topic-based approaches, "*topic work was an important and integral part of the curriculum in schools where there was good practice* (in history and geography); *it was the major vehicle for promoting history, geography, science and, in many cases, several other subjects.*" (DES)

From pluralism to centralism

In its pluralistic form at least three faces of geography could be discerned in addition to its traditional regionalism:

the scientific/positivist face:

> "'*Geography as science*' *is characterised by its abstraction and modelling of reality, and it has made tremendous contributions to the development and rigour of geography in schools through its power to engage and strengthen reasoning skills.*" (Slater, 1982, p. 1)

the humanistic face:

> "'*Geography as personal environmental response*' *directs attention to our experiences and interpretations of everyday life, whether structured cognitively or emotionally...*" (Slater)

the radical/welfare face:

> "*Through studying space and society, geography can encourage students to be critical... of the ideology that guarantees the persistence of inequalities in material and social wellbeing.*" (Lambert, 1992, p.159)

In 1985 Sir Keith Joseph, the then Secretary of State for Education, posed seven questions about geography as a school subject to the Geographical Association (GA), resulting in the publication by the Geographical Association (GA) of *A Case for Geography* (Bailey and Binns, 1987) containing a developed response to the seven questions. The GA's response is generally held to have secured the place of geography in Kenneth Baker's 'broad and balanced entitlement' view of the centrally-determined and legally enforced National Curriculum 5 to 16, though the situation has changed somewhat with geography no longer being required at key stage 4.

This brings us to the definition of geography advanced by the Geography National Curriculum Working Group and quoted earlier. It should be noted that the processes around the development of the National Curriculum in general, and the Order for geography in particular, were controversial - see, for instance the letter quoted in the margin. The then Secretary of State Kenneth Clarke amended the documents for history and geography, acting with a single political adviser over the Christmas holiday of 1990-1, making substantial changes before the Draft Orders were published. Knowledge was given greater emphasis; skills and explorations of attitudes and values, less.

Activity

1. Contrast the views expressed in the letter (see margin) with the following comments:

   "*Kenneth Clarke took a knife to the proposals, hacking out controversial issues and aspects of enquiry.*" (Morgan, 1994, p. 32)

   "*In respect of their views on the nature and purpose of geography, the Orders reflect the failure to consider integration within the subject, as well as between subjects.*" (Morris, 1992, p. 78)

   "*Radical teachers will do their best with it in the interests of their pupils, but they should continue to refine and work for alternatives.*" (Huckle, 1991, p. 117)

2. Identify the value-positions underlying the letter and the comments quoted above.
3. What underlying values about the nature of geography would you want embodied in the National Curriculum?
4. What is your own position on the principle (as opposed to the content) of a Geography National Curriculum? Should there be such a thing, or should it be left to teachers? Justify your position.
5. It would be useful to discuss your responses to these issues with your peer partner.

Geography as others teach it

In exactly the same way as I have suggested that your perception of what it means to teach geography is the product of your experience, the same is true for those we might call experienced teachers of geography. They, of course, have had additional experiences in the role of teacher of geography to further develop their view of the subject. They will differ from one another, however, in many ways, including their personal theories of geography and how to teach it. These personal theories will be implicit in the teaching they actually do, and this teaching can be observed directly by you.

Activity

1. Arrange to observe three lessons in which some geography will be taught. This will of course be straightforward in a context where single subject geography takes place, but may require some forethought and planning in a topic-based or interdisciplinary context.
2. Before each lesson, try to find time with the teacher for them to tell you what is planned for the lesson as regards the subject of geography. It may be that they will have a written lesson plan to which you can refer. If not, make a note of their intentions. Ask them how they will evaluate the lesson.
3. Observe the lesson. Concentrate on the teacher and what s/he says and does. Make notes about the geography teaching which takes place.
4. After each lesson, reflect on what you observed and the notes you made. Consider the following questions:
   - What relationship did the lesson 'as taught' bear to the teacher's original intentions, and to what extent were those intentions/objectives realised?

Humanities halted

"*Mr Pattinson in his letter ('Humanities fall prey to political manipulation', February 1) complains that geography and history syllabuses have been subject to political manipulation by the Secretary of State. I would argue that the political manipulation of geography and history happened a lot earlier and came from a very different quarter - that of the 'humanities' lobby - whose sole aim over the years has been to undermine geography and history syllabuses through the teaching of such 'subjects' as inequality, poverty, apartheid and community politics. Well done Mr Clarke for recognising the spreading cancer of 'humanities' and for returning geography and history to their true and respected disciplines.*"

Elizabeth Hodder (Letter to 'Times Educational Supplement', 15th Feb. 1991)

In Beginning Teaching Workbook 2 it was suggested that you keep a diary or 'reflective journal' detailing your experiences. The reflective part of this activity could be written up in such a journal.

- What geography teaching did you observe, and what relationship did it bear to your own personal theories about geography and how to teach it?
- On the basis of what you observed, what tentative conclusions can you draw regarding the teacher's own personal theories about geography and how to teach it?
- What questions do you now want to ask the teacher about the geography teaching you observed?

Review

1. In this Chapter you have revisited your previous experiences in geography. You have also looked at something of the development of the subject, and have conducted some observations of geography teaching in action.

2. In the light of the above, conduct a SWOT analysis (strengths / weaknesses / opportunities / threats) of your position vis-a-vis the teaching of geography on the framework, **Figure 2.2**.

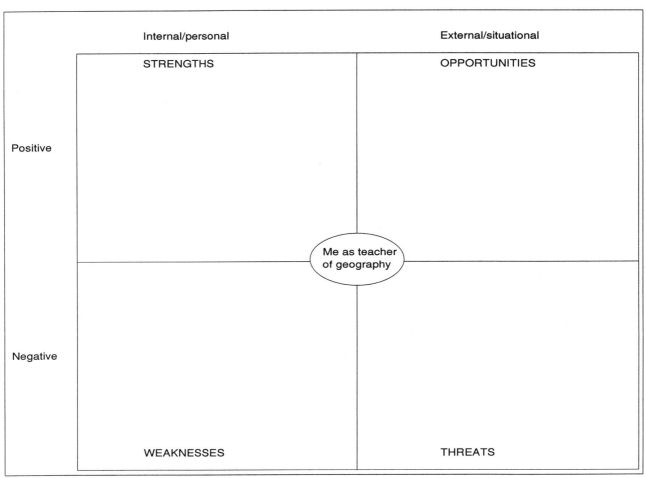

Figure 2.2 Framework for carrying out a SWOT analysis

Again, it may be useful to discuss aspects of the action planning process with another person. This could be a peer partner, a mentor or a 'critical friend'. What's important is that you feel comfortable discussing personal aspects of how you see yourself in relation to your work with them.

3. Consider the results of your analysis. The analysis is not an end in itself. It is the basis for **action planning**. In particular, how do you propose to:
   - *make best use of your strengths;*
   - *take advantage of the opportunities;*
   - *remedy any weaknesses;*
   - *tackle and/or minimise any threats?*

4. Try to write an action plan which identifies:
   - *particular targets;*
   - *the date by which such targets will have been met;*
   - *the criteria by which you will judge their achievement.*

3

Planning and the geography curriculum

"A man, a plan, a canal: Panama" *(historical-geographical palindrome)*

Aims

To be able to plan effectively is fundamental to your development as a teacher. Initially you will associate the word 'planning', naturally enough, with learning activities, lessons, topics and schemes of work. However, the ongoing, cyclical process of planning, doing and reviewing actually characterises all aspects of the work of a school, including its day-to-day running, special events and its long-term development as an institution.

The aims of this Chapter are:

- *to consider the nature of the planning process itself in more detail;*
- *to support you in developing the planning which you will undertake in order to provide for learning in geography;*
- *to link the planning process with external requirements, eg the National Curriculum for geography.*

The planning process

Initially, planning will take you a considerable amount of time (particularly if you are doing it properly!). You may also want to discuss your tentative plans with others, for instance your mentor if you are a student teacher, or another colleague or peer partner if you are newly qualified. As time goes on you will become faster at planning as you internalise the stages in the process, a range of detailed considerations related to your particular circumstances, and a repertoire of alternative approaches for how to go about your work. Thus experienced teachers can do much of their lesson planning quickly, in their heads. freeing time to take on other aspects of the work of the school. This of course is just as well, or all sorts of other things simply would not happen.

When developing your approach to planning, do not try to cut corners! The old adage about not running before you can walk has meaning here. In the early stages of your development it is important to plan methodically and carefully in order to achieve the internalisation of the process described above. Spontaneous ideas may sometimes work brilliantly, but they can also go badly wrong, particularly if you do not have a lot of experience on which to draw. They are also inherently difficult to evaluate systematically - and can make you a difficult colleague with whom to work as you could be something of a maverick! This is particularly so in circumstances where systematic coverage of an agreed curriculum and co-operation over the use of resources are required.

Planning is not an isolated action. It is part of a dynamic, on-going, cyclical process of 'planning, doing and reviewing', represented in **Figure 3.1**. It is also not an isolated action in the sense that it is often undertaken in collaboration with other colleagues.

To the 'person in the street' planning is an invisible and easily overlooked aspect of teaching. As your planning capabilities improve you will experience a 'learning curve'. The full learning curve takes a learner from 'unconscious incompetence' ('I don't know I can't') through conscious phases to 'unconscious competence' ('I can without thinking'). This will apply to many aspects of your 'professional learning' as a teacher. See Beginning Teaching Workbook 2 (pages 6-7) for more about the idea of learning curves and stages in your professional development.

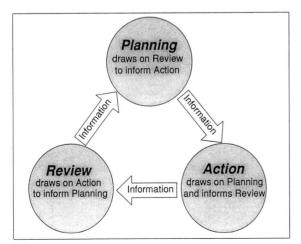

Figure 3.1 Planning as part of a cyclical process

The purpose of planning is to provide a secure basis for action, but it is not possible to plan without making retrospective use of earlier ideas and experiences, hence some of the activities in the previous Chapter. The diagram also indicates that in order for the three phases of the cycle to be linked effectively, it is necessary for **information** to flow round the cycle. This is vital, and the more this flow of information takes place at a conscious, deliberative level, the more secure will be the connections between the phases of the cycle.

In fact there are three main time-scales over which the cycle operates:

- *during the planned action, eg a lesson;*
- *between planned actions, eg from one lesson to the next;*
- *the long term, eg when a topic is repeated another year.*

The first time-scale involves what Schön called 'reflection in action' (see Chapter 1). You approach a lesson with a clear set of intentions (learning objectives) and a clear idea of how you are going to achieve your intentions. However, as the lesson proceeds (the 'action' phase of the cycle) you realise that aspects of the lesson are not going according to plan. You quickly review the situation, gathering information from how individuals are progressing with the activities you have set up, levels of motivation and so on. You adjust the plan, perhaps to change the sequence of activities you had planned, perhaps to identify a small group with whom you will work separately.

The second time-scale involves Schön's 'reflection on action' and is done after the action is completed. Thus it is possible to review the action and the planning which preceded it in a more deliberative and systematic, searching fashion than in the above example. Some questions you might use in this evaluation stage are:

- *Were the objectives appropriate to the ability levels of the various class members?*
- *What levels of enjoyment and interest were evident?*
- *Did some children need more intensive help and others more demanding activities?*
- *Were all objectives achieved or are some objectives to be incorporated into the next lesson?*
- *How did your actions in the lesson appear to assist the learning outcomes you were seeking?*
- *What have **you** learnt from planning, doing and reflecting?*
- *What will you do next, as a result of your reflections?*

See Beginning Teaching Workbook 3 for more on questioning skills. Also Brown and Wragg, (1993).

Some aspects of your professional development, being of a generic nature, are open to scrutiny over this time-scale, for instance questioning skills, which you may plan to use, evaluate and develop over a particular sequence of lessons.

The third time-scale is to do with the long-term cyclical nature of teaching. You plan some learning for a particular group of young people and, eventually, you find yourself back in a similar position with a different group. This may be a year later, or even several years later if you 'move up' with a class. Documented evaluation and review are very important in this context. It is extremely difficult, if not impossible, to recapture your thoughts, feelings and impressions after a year or more has gone by in order to incorporate them into the next planning phase, however vivid, vital and obvious they may have seemed at the time! Clearly, however, your professional development has a very important association with these underlying, long term cycles.

In this Chapter we will concentrate on the second of these three time-scales for the very good reason that the planning you are currently contemplating is in most cases for the first time, and you will want it to be as effective and as securely-based as possible. It is an area of competence you are currently seeking to develop. In the context of this book you will address the issue of planning for learning in geography, but of course, through planning for learning in geography, you will develop a planning competence which can be applied in other circumstances. In the longer term your general ability to plan effectively will be vital to your promotion to posts involving management responsibility, should you seek this.

Planning for learning in geography (i) - the aims of geography

Much of what I have said so far about planning applies to planning in general. But we should now address the question, "What is there that is *particular to geography* which should be borne in mind in the process of planning?"

An uninformed view would be that the purpose of geography is to know facts about places. Few would dispute that place knowledge is an important component of geography, but though it may be necessary, it is far from being a sufficient condition for the subject. This would reduce geography to the status of general knowledge of the Trivial Pursuit variety, but someone who is a walking encyclopedia of this sort of information can no more be said to know geography than someone who can name every star in the sky can be said to know astronomy. So, what is the purpose of geography?

Before you read the remainder of this page you may like to brainstorm and jot down your own understanding of the aims and purpose of geography in order to compare your views with those of HMI.

In the Geographical Association's *A Case for Geography* the question is answered thus: "*The purpose of teaching geography is to enable the growing child and young adult to conceptualise and set in order the dimension of space in which all human beings live.*" (Bailey and Binns, 1987)

In their series *Curriculum Matters* Her Majesty's Inspectorate (HMI) identified the following ten aims for geography in primary and secondary education. They felt that "*geographical studies over the 5 to 16 age range should help pupils to:*

- *develop a strong interest in their own surroundings and in the world as the home of mankind (sic);*
- *appreciate the variety of physical and human conditions on the earth's surface;*
- *recognise some of the more important geographical patterns and relationships which are revealed in different types of landscape and different human activities;*
- *understand some of the relationships between people and environments;*
- *appreciate the importance of geographical location in human affairs and understand how activities and places are linked by movements of people, materials and information, and by complex economic, social, political and physical relationships;*
- *understand what it means to live in one place rather than another;*
- *understand some of the more important physical and human processes which produce geographical pattern and variety and which bring about changes;*
- *develop a range of skills and competences necessary to carry out geographical enquiry and to interpret geographical information;*
- *appreciate the significance of peoples's beliefs, attitudes and values to those relationships and issues which have a geographical dimension;*
- *construct a framework of knowledge and understanding about their home area, about their own country and about other parts of the world, which will enable them to place information within appropriate geographical contexts.*"

HMI, 1986, pages 1-2

Activity

1. Review the above list of aims for geography. Are there any which surprise you? Do you feel that you share these aims for your teaching of geography? Are there any aims which you feel are important, but which do not appear in this list?
2. In Chapter 1, one of the activities suggested you get a copy of the aims and objectives for geography in the school in which you are placed or working. If you were able to do so, compare the school's aims for geography with the HMI view. Are there significant differences and, if so, why do you think this is?

Planning for learning in geography (ii) - skills, places and themes

Once clear about the aims of geography and therefore the purpose of our planning, the next stage is to consider the nature of the component parts which we will attempt to bring into our planning. In England and Wales the development of a National Curriculum Order for geography clearly gives us a statutory minimum which must be covered in the geography curriculum.

In their deliberations the working group identified a tripartite foundation for geography as a subject. Geography comprised, they felt:

- *distinctive **skills** which should be acquired and developed;*
- *knowledge about and understanding of **places / areas**;*
- *knowledge about and understanding of geographical **themes**.*

These aspects, though separable for the purposes of thinking about the subject and its constituent parts, would normally be planned for in combination. This interrelatedness has been expressed as the three visible faces of a cube, as shown in **Figure 3.2.** (DES,1990, p.47)

Figure 3.2 The geography cube

The implication of the cube is that geography only exists when all three elements are present in combination. The subsequent editing of the Order for geography, its modification by the Secretary of State referred to in the previous Chapter and its redrafting after the Dearing Review of 1993 have all left this underlying structure in place, though the amounts of detail prescribed under each of the categories and the assessment structure have changed greatly.

Activity (1)

1. Look at a copy of the programme of study for geography related to the key stage in which you are working. Read the programme carefully.
2. What do you think might be the planning issues for the teacher which stem from this programme of study?

The phrase 'study unit' is borrowed from the history National Curriculum, in which the programme of study for key stages 2 and 3 is divided up into history study units, each with a distinctive focus (a theme or a time period). Within each study unit certain 'key elements' of history (for instance, an enquiry approach and an understanding of chronology) will normally be present, ensuring continuity and progression between study units.

Even a quick glance at the programme of study for geography reveals the planning challenge facing the teacher. Basically the programme of study for each key stage is simply a list of what must be covered. The challenge is to re-order and combine the elements of the list in such a way as to create interesting, cohesive topics or **'study units'** in geography, each with skill, place and thematic dimensions. A carefully planned sequence of such study units will not only ensure coverage of the full programme of study, but also provide for continuity of learning experience and progression across a key stage.

Such a geography study unit will represent a unique combination of thematic knowledge and understanding, place knowledge and understanding, and skills. In this way such a study unit will represent a location somewhere inside the geography cube. The 'coordinates' of this location within the cube would be expressed in terms of skills, places and themes, as shown by **Figure 3.3**. Each of the elements of the programme of study is coded with numbers and letters, to make it easier to cross-refer between a teacher's plans and the programme itself.

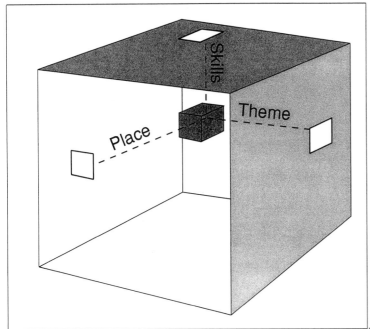

Figure 3.3 The relationship between a 'geography study unit' (shown by the inner cube) **and the programme of study** (outer cube)

I have said above that this is a 'planning challenge', and this is true. But it is also an **opportunity**, in that each school, in planning its approach to geography, can take account of:

- *its locality and what the local area has to offer;*
- *its young people, their needs, abilities and interests;*
- *its resources;*
- *the interests and strengths of its staff;*
- *any links the school may have with the local community;*
- *any links the school may have with other places (eg exchange visits, fieldwork, penfriends);*
- *topicality of issues.*

Indeed, there is no reason why any two schools should go about their geography in quite the same way!

This is particularly the case when we bear in mind that what is specified in the National Curriculum should be seen as a **statutory minimum**, with opportunities for each school to add to the minimum in the light of the points in the above list.

Activity (2)

1. Look again at the relevant programme of study for the key stage with which you are to be working. Conduct a personal 'audit' of your level of familiarity with the National Curriculum requirement for geography. Use the following coding system to indicate your level of familiarity with the elements of the programme of study:
    1 you have knowledge and understanding well beyond the level required;
    2 you have knowledge and understanding adequate for the level required;
    3 your knowledge and understanding are not adequate for the level required;
    4 you have no knowledge and understanding of this element at all.
2. Pick a thematic element you have graded **1** or **2**. Think about a suitable place context in which to set it, and some way/s in which it could contribute to skill development. You have the basis of a geography study unit!
3. Make a note of this embryo study unit - we shall return to it shortly.
4. Do not ignore the aspects of the programme of study which you graded at **3** and **4**. What do you propose to do about these gaps in your knowledge and understanding? Keep the results of this personal audit for future reference.

The doughnut principle
*In his book **The Empty Raincoat** Charles Handy describes what he calls the doughnut principle. The doughnut in question is of the American type, like a bagel: a ring of dough with a hole in the middle. The doughnut principle employs a conceptual doughnut in which the space surrounds the dough. It is, Handy says, "one for thinking with, not for eating." (1994, p.65) In your geography teaching the dough, the core, is the things you have to do in order to fulfil your duty. The National Curriculum is in the core. But to really be **a teacher of geography** and, beyond that, **a teacher of children**, you have to go beyond the core into the space. "This space" says Handy "is our opportunity to make a difference, to go beyond the bounds of duty, to live up to our full potential. That remains our ultimate responsibility in life, a responsibility which is always larger than our duty, just as the doughnut is larger than its core." (p.66)*

Planning for learning in geography (iii) - the geography lesson

> "Planning for the teaching of geography, like all subjects, must inevitably incorporate an understanding of what the learners already know, that is, what they are bringing to the learning situation, and the related ability of a teacher to find this out and to develop it."

Palmer, 1994, p. 52

To some degree a well-planned lesson in geography is just like a well-planned lesson in anything else. It will normally have:

- *a clear purpose in the form of explicit objectives (intended learning outcomes);*
- *relevance and a clear, explicitly stated relationship to previous and subsequent learning;*
- *an appropriate structure, (eg a teacher-led introduction, a sequence of learning activities, a concluding discussion to review and consolidate learning);*
- *realistic time allocations to the elements of the structure;*
- *appropriate provision for differentiation according to individual needs;*
- *resources (including room and furniture arrangement, as well as subject resources, materials and teaching aids) to support the intended learning outcomes;*
- *provision for evaluation and/or assessment.*

In the early stages of becoming a teacher, to do this sort of planning properly is, as noted in the introduction to this Chapter, time-consuming but very important. Most beginner teachers build up a file of lesson plans which, as well as documenting one aspect of progress as a teacher, provide a basis for future work, thereby getting the maximum return on the large amount of time invested in the process.

There is more detail about objectives in Chapter 4 where a substantial section examines the nature of objectives as 'intended learning outcomes' in geography.

In the particular case of geography we can see that the subject provides a specific context in which the above generally applicable criteria will be manifest. Thus the lesson objectives, for instance, will make specific reference to aspects of geography, blending if possible aspects of skill development with the extension of thematic knowledge and understanding in a place context. The nature of the learning activities and the resources utilised will reflect the subject orientation of the objectives set.

It is important to stress that planning is not an activity to be undertaken in isolation. It is an activity which, to be truly effective, must consider real learners in a real context, as indicated by the quotation at the start of this section. There are also benefits to be derived from planning collaboratively, with colleagues acting as 'critical friends' and contributing alternative ideas.

Activity

1. Read the following paragraph, taken from an OFSTED inspector's report of a Year 7 mixed ability geography lesson:

   "Aim for lesson outlined and routines quickly established, with high expectations for work and behaviour. The task set (on the local area) was purposeful and the teacher used praise and encouragement well. The task was well structured to allow opportunities for sustained writing and to draw ideas together. The homework activity follows on, involving personal research and the practising of practical investigative skills. Effective teaching based on good knowledge and understanding of the local area. Grade 1."

   OFSTED, 1995, p.18

2. Try to imagine the lesson from the inspector's description, and then consider the following questions:
   - What did the teacher do well?
   - What knowledge and understanding did the teacher have to enable him/her to do these things effectively?
   - What specific planning will the teacher have carried out in order for this lesson to have been so successful?

Planning for learning in geography (iv) - enquiry

"The acquisition of geographical knowledge involves much more than the memorisation of information. A well developed geographical understanding can only result from a process of enquiry in which questions are asked, evidence is examined and conclusions reached."

Northern Ireland Council for Educational Development (NICED), 1988

Our attention so far has been focused largely on the 'what' of planning for learning in geography. This is reflected in statements of competence which focus on 'subject knowledge'. But the 'how' is just as important. The programme of study of the National Curriculum for England and Wales specifies the use of an enquiry approach. Though this will have been a case of 'preaching to the converted' for some teachers of geography, for whom such an approach already characterised their work, it is nevertheless useful in giving a clear lead by formalising enquiry as a requirement rather than simply being desirable. Once again, however, this leaves questions for the teacher to consider:

In the National Curriculum programme of study for England and Wales enquiry is evident in elements 1a and b, element 2 (skills) and by reference to 'investigation' in element 6 (themes). This is so for all key stages.

- *What is an 'enquiry approach'?*
- *How can I plan for an 'enquiry approach'?*
- *What is the balance between autonomy and direction in the 'enquiry approach'?*

What is an 'enquiry approach'?

The enquiry approach is not a single, fixed pathway. It can be thought of as a questioning orientation towards the subject, resulting in a spectrum of 'finding out', with at one end perhaps a single question with a single, verifiable answer and, at the other, a lengthy procedure of several stages in order to test a hypothesis. In general it is helpful to think of enquiry in geography as a sequence of linked questions which provide knowledge, understanding, clarification and, sometimes, further questions. At times it will move from the specific aspects of the case in point to some form of generalisation - a tentative theory of some sort.

A hypothesis is a statement which is open to test or verification through an investigation. 'The road outside our school is busier in the morning than in the afternoon' is a hypothesis. An investigation could be conducted to find out whether the statement is true or not, and explanations could be advanced for whatever is discovered.

An important feature of an enquiry sequence is that it develops thinking skills in the learner. Though facts of some sort are a necessary component of an enquiry, they are not an end in themselves in the development of higher order thinking skills. A series of closed questions which simply yield, consolidate or recall factual knowledge without moving on to higher thinking levels will not develop thinking skills. Thus enquiry needs an investigative, open-ended orientation to the sequence of questions. Clearly as teacher your understanding of the enquiry approach and its role is important, as it will determine how you go about your planning.

The developers of *The Queensland Geography Syllabus* identified four guiding questions for geographical investigation:

- *Where are things located?*
- *Why are they there?*
- *What are the consequences of their location?*
- *What alternative locations may be considered in decision making? (Slater, 1982, p.5)*

The 16 - 19 Geography Project put it slightly differently in an issue-based approach to enquiry:

- *Identify a geographical issue through knowledge and observation ;*
- *Define and describe the situation in which the issue is manifest;*
- *Analyse and explain aspects of the issue;*
- *Evaluate the implications and predict consequences;*
- *If appropriate, identify decisions to be taken.*

Both of these approaches are located within the 'positivist' approach to geography which deals with a supposedly objectively verifiable, factual world. The authors of *The 16 - 19 Project* also identified the possibility of conducting 'values enquiry' in which individuals' subjective views about an issue would themselves be the focus of the enquiry. This could be run in parallel with the more objective, factual enquiry. Both involve progression through levels of thinking, as we can see by comparing them to the cognitive levels of Bloom's classification shown in **Figure 3.4**

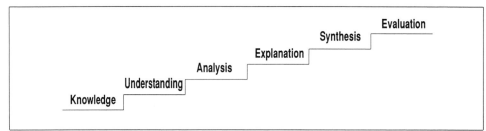

Figure 3.4 Bloom's hierarchy of cognitive levels

The Geographical Association (1991) suggested the following questions to be applied to place or thematic enquiries:

- *What is it? Where is it? What is it like? What is it about?*
- *How did it get like this? How and why did it happen? What processes are involved? With what effect?*
- *What might happen? With what impacts? What decisions will be made? With what consequences?*
- *What do people think and feel about this? Why? What do I think and feel? What next?*

Judy Sebba (1995, p.1) suggests the following list of questions to guide place-oriented enquiry:

- *What is this place like?*
- *Where is this place in relation to where I live or other places I know?*
- *How is it similar to, or different from, other places?*
- *How is this place changing?*
- *What would it be like to be in this place?*
- *What do I like about this place?*
- *How is this place connected to other places?*

These questions are similar to those given in the National Curriculum programme of study, but go a step further. We can see that in this sequence the learner's **private geography** is also explicitly brought into the frame. A private geography, following the work of David Lowenthal, is each individual's personalised collection of knowledge about the world of physical phenomena (the human and natural environments) and the values the individual holds towards the world as he or she knows it. Though there is shared knowledge and understanding about the world (eg most would agree on the distinction between say, land, sea and air), each person's experiences are to some degree unique, and thus it follows that, as each has an individual experience of being-in-the-world, so each will have a 'private geography'.

The above list of questions taps into this private geography with questions directed at experience, empathy and preference. This has the effect of linking the cognitive and affective domains in what has been called 'confluent education'. (Fien, 1983, p.49) The two currents which are 'flowing together' are the current of cognition involving 'objective' enquiry about the world of physical phenomena and the affective current involving the subjective, personal, value-conditioned response to that world. In this way, geographical enquiry is not just about the world 'out there' but also about our individual interactions with it and, as a consequence, has a strong values dimension, heightening its relevance and educational potential. Thus:

> *"Geographical enquiries are likely to give rise to debate about issues such as changing land-use and pressure on natural resources. Encouraging pupils to consider opposing views, and different values and attitudes, can be helpful in promoting respect for diversity of opinion, an essential feature of a democratic society."*

> *National Curriculum Council, 1991*

How can I plan for an 'enquiry approach'?

Having clarified something of what is meant by 'enquiry' we now turn our attention to the second of the questions with which we began this section. At one level planning for enquiry means setting out to ask questions of those whom you are teaching, instead of just telling them things! It is of course possible to have a token enquiry approach, in which the teacher asks all the questions **and** provides all the answers. Such a rhetorical non-dialogue is of course not what is envisaged when enquiry is described; through undertaking enquiry learners should develop their ability to frame their own questions and, ultimately, conduct their own enquiries. So, normally when we are describing enquiry in the teaching of geography, it is not just a 'question-driven' approach that we have in mind. We are also thinking about **active learning** and experiential learning.

Active learning is explored in greater detail in Chapter 5, particularly pages 50-51.

At one level there need be no mystique around the idea of active learning. It simply describes a situation in which learning takes place because the learner is engaged in doing something. The rationale is summed up in the oft-quoted (in education and training circles at least) Chinese proverb, "I hear and I forget, I see and I remember, I do and I understand". The challenge for the teacher is to plan learning activities which satisfy the following conditions:

- *relevance;*
- *manageability;*
- *lead to the desired learning outcomes;*
- *allow for differentiation, continuity and progression.*

The enquiry approach provides a useful framework which, whilst not guaranteeing that the above conditions will be met, at least offers a simple structure within which to plan for active learning. It also provides a linking thread for activities. The enquiry approach can be summarised diagramatically, as in **Figure 3.5.**

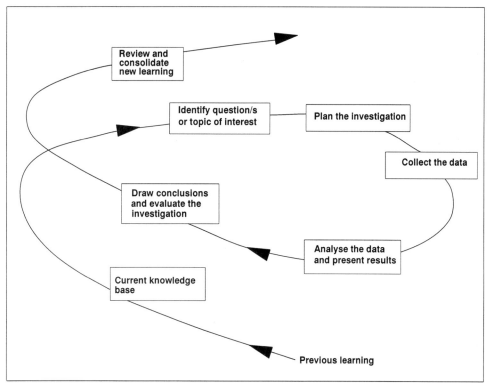

Figure 3.5 The enquiry approach

Sometimes an enquiry can be concluded in a single lesson or even part of a lesson. Other enquiries may last much longer. In order to develop your planning in geography it is important to model the enquiry process by structuring your work around the stages of the process. Thus your planning sequence will be as follows:

- *identify relevant aspect/s of scheme of work or programme of study;*
- *consider how to tackle the chosen aspect/s via an investigative approach;*
- *write a set of objectives for your enquiry;*
- *devise a sequence of questions reflecting the steps or stages of the investigation;*
- *devise a sequence of activities which address the questions.*

Autonomy and direction within the enquiry approach

Once again, rather than imagining a polarised, 'either/or' situation it is more helpful to think of a spectrum of autonomy as illustrated in **Figure 3.6,** in which the balance between autonomy and direction is located somewhere along the spectrum. The balance to be adopted for any particular enquiry will be for you to decide in the light of circumstances and context, including the nature of the work, and what you already know about the students and their capabilities.

The original non-statutory guidance issued by the then Curriculum Council for Wales, (now ACAC), gives some very helpful examples of how to structure enquiries in geography (1991, pages 41 - 46). The examples are based around the Geographical Association's suggested questions (see margin, previous page).

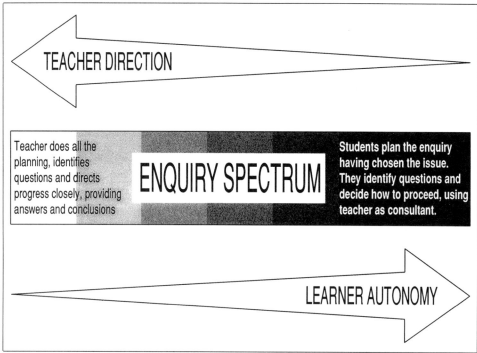

Figure 3.6 Geographical enquiry - the balance between direction and autonomy

In the planning sequence described in the previous section, most decisions about the progress of the enquiry are taken by the teacher. There is limited room for individual autonomy on the part of learners. On the other hand it is possible for the teacher to decide that some or all of the stages summarised by the second, third and fourth bullet points could be handed over to individuals or groups who would then identify their own questions and decide how to proceed. However, it is important to remember that natural inquisitiveness is not the same thing as a grasp of what it means to systematically and rigorously investigate something, so most children will need guidance to a certain extent in carrying out the stages of an enquiry. For this reason it is important that you as teacher provide a rôle model by adopting an enquiry approach in your planning and by demonstrating an approach which is both questioning and question-driven.

Of course, geography is not unique in utilising an enquiry approach. Kenyon (1994, p.122) notes how the enquiry approach can integrate work at key stage 2 involving aspects of geography, mathematics and science. He gives a fully developed example of such an integrated investigation, used with a Year 5 class. Marsden (1994, p.110) identifies commonality in approaches to enquiry between geography and history. The primary school teacher of geography is well placed to make the most of these and other connections.

Planning for progression in geographical enquiry can involve some or all of:

- *increasing levels of autonomy;*
- *more sophisticated or searching questions;*
- *the use of more complex or more sophisticated concepts and techniques;*
- *more variables to consider;*
- *increasing degree of unfamiliarity of context of enquiry.*

Such connections exist at the secondary level as well, though it is sometimes more difficult to capitalise on the opportunity for integration of the planning of geography with other subjects due to the structuring of the timetable around separate subjects with different teachers. It is then a matter of liaison between subject departments to ensure that, where possible, work can be mutually reinforcing, and that subject teachers know what is going on in other areas of the curriculum so that they can support learners in seeing and exploiting the links. Clearly it is undesirable for there to be no communication, and for subject learning to be seen by teachers and students alike as compartmentalised and unconnected.

The cross-curricular development of enquiry skills is important, and an enquiry in geography can, particularly at A Level, draw on knowledge, skills and understanding developed in other curriculum areas.

Activity

1. Look back at the bulleted list of stages in the planning of a geographical enquiry (see p.23). Plan an enquiry following these stages; ideally it will be one you intend to teach, rather than merely a 'paper exercise'. If possible, use the outline study unit from the previous section as the context for the enquiry. (If you are undertaking this activity as a student teacher you may need to do the first stage in consultation with your mentor.)

2. Before you undertake the detailed planning of activities, consult your mentor, head of department or subject coordinator about the outline of your enquiry, the questions around which you are structuring it and the nature of the activities in which you want your students to be involved. In the light of your discussion, evaluate and, if necessary, amend your plans.
3. Identify and discuss the criteria against which you will evaluate your enquiry once it is concluded. (If you are not in a position to teach your enquiry stop at this point!)
4. Plan and prepare in the normal way (eg by drawing up a sequence of lesson plans and by devising and assembling appropriate materials) for the learning activities which form your enquiry sequence.
5. Teach the sequence.
6. Evaluate your enquiry against the evaluation criteria which you identified earlier.

Planning for learning in geography (v) - schemes of work and the key stage plan

So far most of our thoughts about planning in geography have been directed at the immediate concern of the single lesson or enquiry sequence. However, planning is about coordination at a number of scales as indicated in **Figure 3.7**

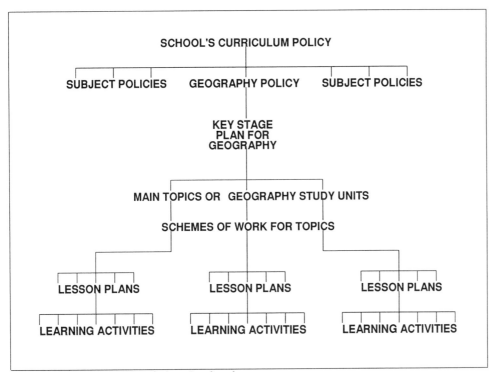

Figure 3.7 The hierarchy of planning levels

The diagram also indicates how the individual classroom learning activity is connected through the levels of the planning hierarchy, to the school's overall curriculum policy as agreed by the school's governing body.

Schemes of work perform an important function, as they show how the teaching of a subject is organised. Thus they provide accessible information both for teachers planning individual lessons and for curriculum managers, governors, parents and inspectors interested in how the school's teaching is organised. As shown in **Figure 3.7**, they are intermediate in detail between a key stage plan, which may be a framework divided into, say, half term sections simply listing the main topics, and lesson plans which detail the amount of time to be allocated to individual learning activities. Thus a scheme of work would typically be organised on a grid such as the one in **Figure 3.8**, (see p.26) in such a way as to enable an overview of a topic or unit, including planned progression in the work. There is no set system of how to draw up schemes of work; each school is free to organise them in its own way.

Topic	....	Year group				
Aims						
Lesson	Key ideas/ objectives	Questions	Activities	Resources	Links (subjects, themes etc)	PoS covered

Figure 3.8 A typical framework for a scheme of work

Further exemplification and discussion of planning for geography at specific key stages can be found in:

- *Fran Martin (1996) Teaching Early Years Geography (pages 23 - 25);*
- *Bill Chambers and Karl Donert (1996) Teaching Geography at Key Stage 2 (pages 22 - 25);*
- *Jeff Battersby (1996) Teaching Geography at Key Stage 3 (pages 17 - 20).*

Activity

1. Critically evaluate the format of your school's schemes of work:
    - Does the school have a preferred format which is used by all teachers?
    - Do the schemes of work fulfil the function of providing an accessible overview?
    - Do they contain enough information, too much, or are they about right in your judgement?
2. Review the schemes of work for geography in your school. How effectively do they:
    - relate to an overall key stage plan?
    - provide a clear context for the planning of individual lessons and/or learning activities?
3. Given a free hand, would you redesign your school's schemes of work? If so, how?
4. To be involved in the planning of schemes of work is an important aspect of your professional development. You should ensure that you have an opportunity to design, teach and evaluate a full scheme of work for a geography study unit, if necessary for a pre-existing topic.

Note

This Chapter has focused on selected aspects of the planning process. Planning also involves considerations which are covered in greater detail in the following four Chapters, for instance teaching and learning styles, differentiation, resources and information technology, assessment and links with other aspects of the curriculum.

4
Teaching for learning in geography

Aims

The previous Chapter concentrated on aspects of planning in geography. Some of these aspects, including the enquiry approach, will continue into this Chapter in which we take a closer look at your professional development from the perspective of the 'action' phase of the planning cycle with which the previous Chapter began (**Figure 3.1**). So, we will concentrate on 'the teaching you' in the interactive, learning situation of the geography lesson. This Chapter therefore has a number of linked aims:

* *to examine what is meant by 'teaching' and 'learning';*
* *to provide a framework for thinking holistically about teaching and learning as interconnected activities;*
* *to examine the nature of objectives as 'intended learning outcomes' in general, and in geography in particular;*
* *to consider aspects of differentiation.*

Teaching

"He who can, does. He who cannot, teaches."

George Bernard Shaw

Though the English-speaking world in general is doubtless greatly blessed that Shaw lived and wrote, the teaching profession has, in those two short sentences, reason to rue the day that Shaw ever learned to write a word! Deceptively simple from the outside, teaching is of course both complex and difficult.

Unfortunately, to many people the word 'teach' is virtually synonymous with 'tell', and the difficult and complex business of teaching for learning is thereby rendered unproblematic and misleadingly straightforward. 'Knowing one's subject' assumes an unwarranted pre-eminence in some discourses about education, and knowledge about that subject becomes the product which the teacher has to 'deliver' by 'telling' (Stones, 1992, p.16). This reductive view of teaching as telling marginalises other important aspects of the subtle and complex interaction between teaching and learning. I am not suggesting that subject knowledge is not important - just that it is but one of a number of important aspects of teacher capability, as indicated for instance in the 'standards' issued by the TTA.

Stones (p.104) draws attention to the 'preactive', 'interactive' and 'evaluative' phases of teaching, which parallel the 'plan-do-review' model which I have emphasised elsewhere (see eg **Figure 3.1**). This underlines the point that not only is teaching more than telling: it is also more than just the interactive / doing phase.

Activity - brainstorming 'teaching'

1. Although you can obviously do this activity on your own, you may find it more interesting to do it with a partner or a small group, either as a cooperative process or individually, in order to be able to compare results.
    * What do you think of when the word 'teaching' is mentioned? What are the images and associations which enter your mind?
    * Jot down the words which you associate with teaching.
    * If appropriate compare your results with those of your partner/s. Discuss any similarities and differences. What are the origins of your associations?
    * Compare your results with **Figure 4.1**.
2. The diagram, **Figure 4.1** summarises some of what we may mean when we talk of teaching. The diagram is not exhaustive; you may want to add elements. Similarly, some of the words may seem synonymous, or nearly so. But the point is made that teaching is indeed complex, particularly so when we remember that, in the normal teaching situation (whatever that is!), the teacher is doing several things at once, each of which can be done well or less well, effectively or less effectively.

Figure 4.1 Some activities included in teaching

Teaching and learning

> "*You can lead a horse to water*
> *but you can't make it drink.*
> *You can send a kid to college*
> *but you can't make him think.*"
>
> *Trad.*

The relationship between teaching and learning is deceptively simple. You teach, they learn, Q.E.D. The diagram (**Figure 4.1**) concentrates on the teacher's actions and activities, but of course unless learning has taken place among the teacher's students one could argue that there has been no true teaching - just miscellaneous activity on the part of the teacher. If nothing has been learnt, can anything *really* have been taught?

Learning, if we follow the line of reasoning above, is a necessary outcome if we are to say that teaching has taken place. However, as many teachers know from experience, what is learnt is not necessarily that which was intended or taught, eg "I showed them my slides of different parts of the city but all they seemed interested in was how out of date the cars and fashions looked." Also, as we know, learning can and does take place in the total absence of teaching! So, the sobering conclusion is that **teaching is neither a necessary nor a sufficient condition for learning**. Yet learning is, after all, the core objective of teaching. This is, to say the least, something of a paradox.

Elliott (1989, p.242) describes a view of teaching in which the purpose is that of **enabling** young people to take responsibility for their own learning. This is in contrast to a formal, input/output view of teaching where desired outcomes are identified, and the most efficient way of yielding those outcomes is applied. The latter view is well and good when recall of memorised information is required, or when what Elliott (p.241) calls 'algorithmic problem solving' (the application of learned rules to the solution of a problem) is needed. But when the aim of teaching is for 'children to develop enquiring minds' or 'learn with understanding' the teacher is not in a position to input such qualities. Rather, the role of the teacher is **to create the conditions for learning.**

> *"When teachers **enable** children to 'develop enquiring minds', to 'learn with understanding' they are not **producing** certain qualities of mind in children, but establishing conditions which provide children with opportunities for developing such qualities. The enabling conditions may obtain even when children fail to realise these qualities in their learning. People can fail to do what others have enabled them to do......*
>
> *One must, therefore, distinguish teaching which exerts **causal influence** on learning, and teaching which exerts an **enabling influence** on learning."*

Elliott, p.242

Both aspects have a place in the teacher's work. In your work in geography there will inevitably be things which you will want to teach in the causal way. However, given the importance of the enquiry approach in geography (see margin note), for much of the time your teaching will consist of setting up and managing the conditions for learning, that is, 'enabling'. (This book itself stands as an example of an enabling approach. A stated aim in the introduction is to support you in becoming autonomous and self-reliant. My writing the book will not, could not, **cause** you to develop these attributes as a teacher of geography. However, it is certainly the intention that the ideas and activities in the book may provide some of the conditions to help you to learn about yourself in the role of teacher in general, and teacher of geography in particular. It is the same in school: if your aim is that young people should become autonomous learners, do not make them over-dependent on you by casting yourself - and their learning - solely in the causal role.)

For more detail about the enquiry approach you are referred to the relevant section of Chapter 3.

Thus in the enabling 'enquiry' approach to geography you will be interested in both the method as an approach, the outcome, however tentative (and more often than not it should be tentative - there are few things as seductively misleading as certainty) and, above all, the thinking that is going on. Thus as a teacher in this situation you will be "engaged in exploring the *way* students think, not what they should think" and as consequence "spending more time listening to students than talking at or to them". (Postman and Weingartner, 1969, p.45) Your goal is

*Germaine Greer, speaking on 'Desert Island Discs' on BBC Radio 4, described how, after the publication of her book **The Female Eunuch**, women would write to her thanking her for writing it and saying that she had changed their lives. She would write back along the lines of "Thank you for reading **The Female Eunuch**. I didn't change your life. YOU did."*

> *"to engage students in those activities which produce knowledge: defining, questioning, observing, generalizing, verifying, applying. Whatever we think we 'know' about astronomy, sociology, chemistry, biology, linguistics etc. was discovered or invented by someone who was more or less an expert in using inductive methods of inquiry. Thus, our inquiry, or 'inductive' teacher is largely interested in helping his (sic) students to become more proficient as users of these methods."*

Postman and Weingartner, pages 45-6

Activity

1. Review a recent geography lesson you have given, or which you observed. Try to identify aspects of causally-oriented teaching and teaching of the enabling type.
2. Think about the relative amount of the two types of teaching identified above.
   What is the balance between them in the lesson in question?
   To what extent would you say this is typical?
3. Are you satisfied with the balance? If not, what do you propose to do about it?

Learning

"A camel is stronger than a man; an elephant is larger; a lion has greater valour; cattle can eat more than a man; birds are more virile. Man was made for the purpose of learning."

El-Ghazali, C12th. (in Shah, 1968, p.62)

'Learning' is difficult to define precisely. It is even more slippery than 'teaching', yet it is a word we use freely, both in and beyond educational circles, as if there were some consensual understanding of its meaning. But look more closely. In some contexts it means rote memorisation of knowledge, in others the deliberate and conscious acquisition of competences, in others again the gradual subconscious association of one behaviour with another through repetition.

In **Workbook Two** of the **Beginning Teaching Workbooks** series we described the learning cycle as conceptualised by David Kolb. Kolb puts experience at the heart of learning, to the extent that the two terms 'learning' and 'experience' are conflated into the phrase 'experiential learning'. Learning is therefore closely bound up with personal development. In a sense, learning takes place through everything an individual does. 'Getting to know' another person is a learning process. So is watching a film. Writing a book is a learning process. But, of course, the learning which is of interest to us here is that which takes place in schools, and in geography lessons in particular.

Learning is difficult to measure directly. OFSTED inspectors make judgements about 'quality of learning' (as well as quality of teaching), but because of the nature of learning as a process such judgements are based on inference from what can be observed directly. The following extract from an OFSTED publication is used to exemplify how inspectors write reports. We can use it here to examine an example of the OFSTED view of learning and how it is depicted by inspectors. The extract is from the geography subject section of a school inspection report.

"Quality of teaching and learning

School A

At key stage 3 the standards of learning are barely satisfactory. Pupils are mostly well behaved but lacked enthusiasm and interest in their work. There was no opportunity for them to discuss ideas with their peers or to undertake geographical enquiry or fieldwork. They experienced a very limited range of teaching methods. In the majority of lessons, pupils were passive learners and made variable progress: but in a Year 8 class a lively discussion about the USA showed how oral work could be developed into good quality writing. At Key Stage 4 the quality of learning was unsatisfactory. Pupils' attitudes to work give cause for concern, particularly in Year 10, where the poor behaviour of some pupils adversely affects the learning of all."

OFSTED, 1995, p.23

Activity

1. Study the above quotation carefully. Identify the main criteria which have been used for making judgements about 'quality of learning'.
2. Critically evaluate the report from the following points of view (bear in mind that the report is a document of public record):
   - the teachers in the department;
   - a Year 10 student;
   - the school's headteacher;
   - a parent with children in the school;
   - a local journalist.
3. Which view of teaching (causal, enabling, or something else) is implicit in this report?
4. Imagine that you are a teacher in the department concerned. What action plan with regard to teaching and learning would you develop as a consequence of receiving this report?

On the relationship between 'learning' and 'development', Fox (1995, pages 57-8) suggests that the meanings of the two terms can be difficult to distinguish. "Learning is used as a more general term, being applied to any example of an enduring change in knowledge, or skill, which results from experience. In this sense learning (from experience) is contrasted with instinct (a biologically built-in way of responding to a problem. 'Learning is also used to describe short-term specific gains in knowledge, whilst 'development' is reserved for longer-term, broader changes in knowledge, skills, attitudes or indeed other mental states."

- *You may find it useful to reflect on your own understanding and use of the two terms.*
- *What usage do you encounter day to day?*

Postman and Weingartner (p. 41-2) offer a number of characteristics displayed by those whom they call 'good learners':

- *confidence in their ability to learn;*
- *enjoyment in solving problems;*
- *confidence in their own judgement;*
- *willingness to be wrong and to modify their position;*
- *not jumping to conclusions;*
- *flexibility and a preference for relativist over absolutist views of knowledge;*
- *respect for facts (and acknowledgement that 'facts' are tentative);*
- *skill in the language behaviours involved in enquiry (questioning, hypothesising etc.)*
- *readiness to accept uncertainty.*

The enquiry method, they contend, helps "learners increase their competence as **learners**. It hopes to accomplish this by having students **do** what effective learners do."

Teaching for learning

"*For every person wishing to teach there are thirty not wanting to be taught.*"

W C Sellar in 'And now all this'

As already noted, the promotion of learning is the core purpose of teaching. And, though he coined a witty aphorism, Sellar actually got it wrong. Young people generally want to learn, and look to the teacher to create and maintain the conditions for learning. In order to 'teach for learning' it is important to know something of the factors which exert an influence on learning so that those factors which are susceptible to modification by the teacher can be manipulated.

Ausubel, quoted by Bennett (1993, p.6) asserted that the single most important factor exerting an influence on learning is what the learner already knows. It follows that the teacher must discover this and "teach accordingly". Whilst acknowledging the underlying truth of this observation, it is important nevertheless to identify other factors which help us to understand the process better.

Bloom, whose hierarchy of cognitive levels we have already used (**Figure 3.4**), produced a simple model of the influences on, and outputs from, a learning activity (**Figure 4.2**). An alternative way of considering the inputs side of Bloom's model is provided by Creemers (1994) (**Figure 4.3**).

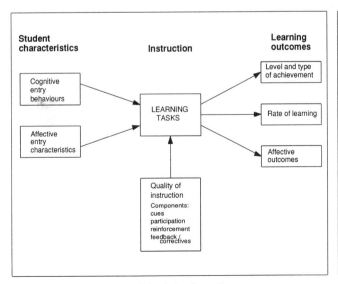

Figure 4.2 Bloom's model of the learning process

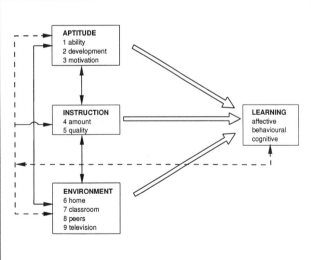

Figure 4.3 Creemers' model of causal influences on the learning processes

In the context of either model, the teacher can obviously influence the nature of the instructional input. (Indeed, a goal of your own professional development will be to enhance this is much as possible.) According to Bloom, this input accounts for up to 25 per cent of the variation in achievement. Creemers also identifies 'instruction' as a distinct variable. A direct influence is also possible, Bloom contends, on the affective variable. In particular, the teacher can capture a learner's enthusiasm and imagination, thereby increasing motivation. Creemers' model implies that in this way a teacher can influence an individual's aptitude towards the learning in question. Motivation, as we shall see below, is important in the influence it exerts on the use made by learners of time and opportunities for learning.

The variable over which the teacher has no direct influence is what Bloom calls 'cognitive entry behaviours'. This variable expresses the learner's cognitive state of readiness to carry out the learning activity in a meaningful way (ie, what the learner already knows, understands and can do), and accounts for between 30 and 60 per cent of the variation in achievement. What this clearly points to is the need for **differentiation**, through which learners are provided with activities (opportunities to learn) which are appropriate to their cognitive entry behaviours. (It would be mistaken to assume that either model therefore requires the use of 'setting' by ability or rigid differentiation by task. But it does point to the need for teachers to be fully aware of individuals' capabilities and prior learning in setting up learning activities for them. This is particularly important when we remember that, in addition to providing for planned differentiation, we also are seeking to ensure continuity and progression in each individuals' learning.)

Creemers argues that in the end two time-related variables mediate all other influences which come to bear on the learning situation:

- *the use learners make of their time for learning;*
- *the use learners make of their opportunities to learn.*

Thus, time 'on task' is vital, both in terms of student motivation, which can itself be influenced by the teacher as we have seen, and also in terms of the amount of time which is made available by the school (timetable) and classroom processes (teacher decisions, distractions, interruptions etc). Time spent on task is only half the story, however.

> "*Time on task is the time in which students are really involved in learning, but this time has to be filled by opportunities to learn*".

Creemers, 1994

It should be remembered that it is possible to be busily engaged in a task, but not actually learning very much. The opportunities to which Creemers refers are **appropriate** learning activities. These reflect the planning decisions and differentiation strategies consciously adopted by the teacher, which in turn reflect the planned objectives (intended learning outcomes) for the particular lesson and the individual child.

Thus we see that in planning and supporting learning in geography, the teacher is working with a complex interplay of three specific types of knowledge:

- ***knowledge about learners:*** *ie the specific children/students with whom the teacher is working, their existing knowledge and understanding, learning capabilities and needs, personal levels of motivation, individual circumstances etc;*
- ***knowledge about geography:*** *as a subject (factual, conceptual and procedural knowledge and understandings) but also including any appropriate National Curriculum programme of study or relevant examination syllabus and knowledge about subject resources;*
- ***pedagogic knowledge:*** *this can be thought of as knowledge about processes of teaching and learning, including the appropriate use of resources. Such knowledge is both general (eg principles of the psychology of learning) and subject-related (eg useful analogies and demonstrations for explaining atmospheric processes when teaching about the weather).*

These three forms of teacher knowledge come into play as components of what we may think of as 'the *teaching and learning* complex'. In this teaching and learning complex, learning in geography is planned and provided for through the teacher's deliberate manipulation of some of the variables which influence the learning process. In this context teaching can be seen as both a causal and an enabling activity which exists for and through the learning process.

This relationship is summarised in the form of a flow diagram, (**Figure 4.4**). The model is dynamic,

Anecdoting

In Develop Your Teaching: a professional development pack for mathematics - and other - teachers (The Mathematical Association, 1991) guidance is given about the use of a process the writers call 'anecdoting' as a way of sharing classroom experiences in such a way as to yield insights leading to professional development.

The process builds on the natural impulse to 'get things off one's chest' or swap 'tales from the classroom'. This has a part to play in dealing with stress, but it also provides opportunities for the identification of real issues. The process can be summarised as:

- *swap anecdotes;*
- *tease out the issues;*
- *agree on action.*

This is a consciously purposeful activity, therefore. Why not try it with a small group of colleagues around the topic of the quotation from Creemers? (See main text)

incorporating the cyclical process of planning / doing / reviewing, operating over a number of time- scales.

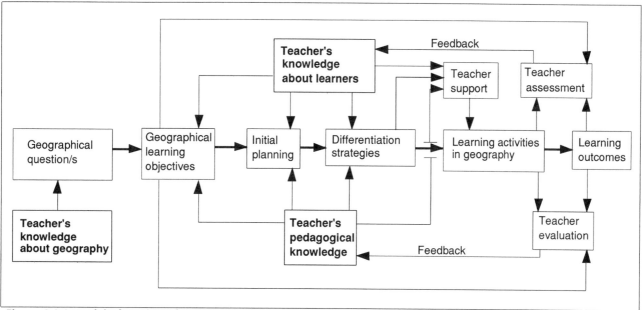

Figure 4.4 A model of teaching for learning in geography

Objectives as intended learning outcomes

Figure 4.4 indicates that, before planning takes place, objectives for learning in geography (amongst others) are set in the light of the question/s which are to be investigated. These objectives play a vital role in the whole process. The objectives themselves reflect your intentions vis-a-vis the subject, but are also influenced by your knowledge about what is necessary, feasible or appropriate for the learners concerned, and by your pedagogical knowledge. Not only do the objectives so identified provide the basis for the planning of the learning to follow, but they also play an important role in the assessment and evaluation processes.

I want to stress that the diagram does not set out to portray the whole picture. The teaching and learning I have attempted to summarise in the diagram is but part of a much larger, more complex picture, itself composed of a myriad of other elements, including:

* **other objectives:** *general, eg the fostering of interest, and cross-curricular, such as the development of problem-solving skills;*
* **other activities:** *eg giving out the letter about the school camp and checking that everyone's book is marked up to date;*
* **other influences:** *eg the 'hidden' curriculum of the school, the values of the peer group, the unique experiences of the individual learner;*
* **other processes:** *eg the unplanned interaction in response to a learner's unforeseen question;*
* **other learning outcomes:** *eg that 'sir' goes on at you if you arrive late to the lesson!.*

Thus the diagram is simply a means to an end - that of unravelling the admitted complexity of it all in order to focus on the particular subject strand in the whole process.

The setting of precise objectives does not come easily to all teachers. Slater (1982, p.18) suggests that the ease with which individuals can set objectives early in the planning process is a reflection of their **cognitive style** and thus their preferred way of going about the planning process. What this means in practice is that you may go from a geographical question to planning the learning activities and then clarify what the objectives are. The objectives are therefore implicit rather than explicit in the early stages of the process. There is research evidence (Clark and Yinger, quoted in Kyriacou, 1991, p.19) to support this view. However, my own teaching experience, particularly when collaboratively planning new schemes of work and their component lessons, was to work from a basis of explicit objectives. What matters is not so much *when* the objectives are explicitly

Your cognitive style is closely connected with your preferred learning style, itself a balance between four tendencies:

* *activist;*
* *reflector;*
* *theorist;*
* *pragmatist.*

This is explored in more detail in **Beginning Teaching Workbook 3** *(Tolley et al, pages 17-20).*

articulated, but that it should happen at some stage before the lesson or activity takes place. What is to be avoided is that the objectives remain only implicit throughout the entire cycle.

In their work on the 'entitlement curriculum' HMI promoted an objectives-led approach, and provided the following definition:

> "Where an **aim** is a general statement of intent, an **objective** was defined as a more specific target which can be realised in practice and assessed with some precision and which is established to help to achieve an aim."

> DES/WO, 1983, p.28

They go on to note that it is helpful to think of objectives in terms of the:

- *skills;*
- *attitudes;*
- *concepts;*
- *knowledge;*

This approach to planning is sometimes referred to by teachers as the SACK or CASK model.

which "are to be taught". Elsewhere (eg DES, 1986, p.2) they refer to the four items in the list as the 'elements of learning', but it is preferable in the context of this discussion of objectives to describe them as the **intended learning outcomes.** We should be clear about what is meant by each. HMI (DES/WO, 1983) define them as follows:

> "**A skill** is a capacity or competence: the ability successfully to perform a task, whether intellectual or manual. The acquisition of a skill may be dependent on the possession of certain knowledge and/or concepts. Skills may be more or less specific; some are applicable in a variety of contexts. Often they hang together in clusters." (p.29)

Map reading skills would be a cluster of skills in geography. Giving a four-figure grid reference would be one of the skills in the cluster. Estimating distance would be another, but would depend on the learner having acquired the concept of scale.

> "**An attitude** is a disposition to think or act in a particular way in relation to oneself and to other individuals or groups in society. Attitudes determine responses to problems, issues and situations." (p.32)

Examples in the case of geography would be empathy with the victims of a natural disaster, or cooperation in the collection of data for an investigation.

> "**A concept** enables one to classify, organise and understand knowledge and experience; often it is the abstraction and generalisation from a number of discrete instances. Concepts may be used for predicting behaviour, for interpreting fresh phenomena and data in a particular field, and for perceiving connections between one area of study and another." (p.32)

I have already mentioned 'scale' as a concept in geography. 'Erosion', 'industry' and 'land use' would be other examples.

> **Knowledge...** "is the information which is selected to develop skills, attitudes and concepts and to achieve aims identified in the curriculum. As well as knowledge selected for this purpose, other knowledge may arise from the spontaneous interests and enthusiasms of both teachers and pupils." (p.33)

We can see that the selection of knowledge by the teacher will be important, not just as information to be acquired in its own right, but also to provide a broad and balanced context for the development of skills, concepts and attitudes. Thus in your planning you will want to provide opportunities for study reflecting the diversity of geographical conditions in different parts of the world, rather than over-dwelling in one region.

It is an important aspect of your own professional development that you develop your ability to set clear, explicit objectives, initially to guide your teaching and its evaluation, but later to play a full part in other aspects of the functioning of a school. In the introduction to Chapter 3 I noted that planning characterises all levels of a school's activity. The same is true of the setting of objectives which seek to respond to questions such as "what do we intend to achieve?" or "what is the purpose of this?" The setting of objectives is a professional competence. It can be consciously learnt and developed.

The objectives-led approach has been subject to some criticism. By their nature, some aspects of geography are more open-ended than others. How, for instance, can meaningful objectives be written for an enquiry where the outcome is either not known, or unpredictable? Part of the answer to this particular question lies in Marshall McLuhan's oft-quoted dictum, "The medium is the message"; that is, one of the primary objectives will be to undertake and evaluate a geographical enquiry *for its own sake*, whatever the focus of the investigation or its apparent outcome. In other words, an enquiry is (or should be) rather more than just an over-elaborate way of simply telling the learner something!

The objectives-led approach has also been criticised for being too inflexible and positivistic in nature. It may be inflexible in the hands of some teachers, but if so I would say that it is the teachers who are inflexible, not the approach! It is important that objectives are not worn as some sort of pedagogical straitjacket. Rather, they should be seen as a point of departure, a set of signposts for possible directions of travel. But we can stop and examine something interesting which happens to crop up *en route* - indeed, it is sometimes very important that we do so. Slater (p.19) notes that we may well modify our initial objectives in the interactive teaching and learning situation but that it is important to start out with a goal in mind. Equally, it is up to the teacher to recognise that not all that happens in the human context of the classroom can or should be accounted for in a series of objectives.

Activity - reflecting on objectives

1. Select a lesson you have planned and taught recently.
2. Critically evaluate your objectives. Were they:
   - explicit?
   - clearly expressed?
   - focused on skills, attitudes, concepts and knowledge?
   - expressed as intended learning outcomes?
   - an appropriate basis for evaluation and assessment?
3. If the answer to any of the above questions is 'no', try to reformulate the objectives in the light of the ideas in the previous section.

Differentiation

Figure 4.4 also makes the place of differentiation clear. Differentiation is both a planning and an active teaching issue. In a way, differentiation in geography is no different (!) from differentiation in any other subject because it is basically to do with matching the opportunities for learning to an individual's abilities (Bloom's 'cognitive entry behaviours'), as noted in the earlier discussion of learning. This could mistakenly be interpreted as different work for each individual, or a huge progressive framework with each learner progressing through it at his/her own speed.

But there would be losses if the entire process were to be individualised. Part of learning is the Vygotskian process of making meaning in geography (and all other subjects and areas of study) through processes of social interaction. Also, lessons, as noted by Kyriacou (1991, p.19) are about social development as well as intellectual development. So another paradox of teaching is revealed: it is important to think about learners as individuals, but there are good reasons for working with them as groups. And of course, we almost invariably do encounter them in groups, often of thirty or so.

The National Curriculum Order for geography for England and Wales places a statutory requirement on teachers to teach the programme of study for each key stage "to all or the great majority of pupils in the key stage, in ways appropriate to their abilities." (DFE, 1995, p.1) By implication this is a requirement for differentiation, in that there is also an implication that the abilities which are referred to will vary from individual to individual. This is borne out by the assumption that at the end of a key stage attainment will be spread across a range of levels of attainment, summarised in the form of 'level descriptions'. Hence, 'ways appropriate to their abilities' will also differ, sometimes at the individual level.

But of course most teachers do not need an Act of Parliament to tell them to differentiate: to them aspects of differentiation are synonymous with good teaching. Much differentiation occurs spontaneously because of teachers' knowledge of individual learners, their attainments, strengths, needs and other attributes. Other differentiation is foreseen and planned for. **Figure 4.5** summarises some aspects of differentiation.

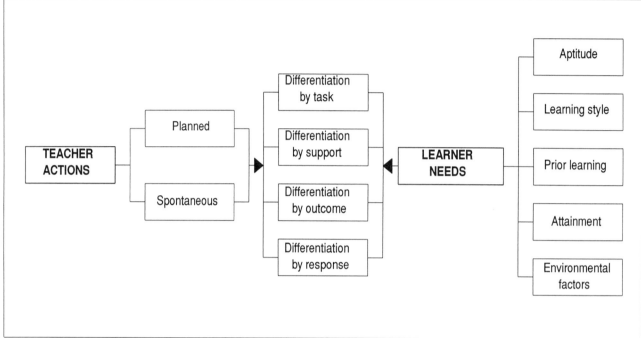

Figure 4.5 Some aspects of differentiation

- **Differentiation by task** is where learners do a task appropriate to their needs and capabilities. This may be self-selected or as directed by the teacher.
- **Differentiation by outcome** is where learners of all levels of ability do the same task, eg draw a map of their route to school. Individuals respond to the task according to their capabilities. The teacher may direct the nature of the outcome or again may allow a choice to be made.
- **Differentiation by support** is sometimes overlooked in discussions about differentiation, unless special support is allocated, eg a classroom assistant or special needs support teacher. Teachers differentiate by support for much of the time that they are interacting with learners on an individual or small group basis. Learners can be more or less forthcoming in indicating a need for support.
- **Differentiation by response** involves the teacher in making a judgement about the standard of work from an individual in the light of knowledge about the individual's capabilities, and communicating a response accordingly.

If you are embarking on this activity as a student teacher, you may be able to enlist the help of the regular class teacher or a student teacher colleague. Their role would be to assist with aspects of the work (supervision, support etc) so that you can pay more attention to your chosen learners without neglecting the rest of the class .

Activity - teaching for learning in geography: a case study

1. Choose a class whom you know well. Identify a geographical theme or topic to last for several lessons.
2. Choose three individual students whom you feel differ in their current approaches to work and their current attainment. Ascertain these individuals' prior learning (NB aspects of this learning may have taken place away from school).
3. With this in mind, set your learning objectives and plan a series of lessons/activities for the class as a whole, making planned provision for differentiation as appropriate.
4. Teach the sequence of lessons/activities.
5. Wherever possible, focus on processes of assessment and evaluation. Try to engage in them consciously, and make notes as appropriate.

6. Reflect on the sequence in order to clarify your thoughts about:
    *   the extent to which the learning objectives have been met by the three selected individuals;
    *   the role of your planned learning activities in the learning which took place;
    *   how the three individual learners appear to learn;
    *   the nature of any factors supporting or inhibiting learning;
    *   whether the learning behaviours of individuals can be generalised in any way;
    *   the nature of your role vis-a-vis the three individuals, including the nature of any differentiation you can identify.
7. It would be appropriate to note some of your thoughts in your reflective journal. It would also be appropriate to discuss the exercise with someone else (eg, peer partner, mentor, supervising tutor, professional tutor as appropriate).

Teaching for learning: the quality geography lesson

> *"Quality...you know what it is, yet you don't know what it is. But that's self-contradictory. But some things **are** better than others, that is, they have more quality. But when you try to say what the quality is, apart from the things that have it, it all goes poof!....What the hell is Quality? What **is** it?"*

> *Pirsig, 1976, p.17*

It is easy to slip into using the term 'quality' non-rigorously, eg "That's a quality piece of work, Sally." But quality demands definition, because the use of the term carries a heavy implication of judgement against some sort of standards or criteria. Many of the sections in this and the previous Chapter have indicated, either directly or implicitly, some of the characteristics which might be appropriate to the 'quality' geography lesson. This is not to say that there is, or should be, such a thing as 'the perfect geography lesson', an archetype to which all teachers of the subject should aspire. However, it is possible to identify some diagnostic characteristics which may be associated with quality in teaching.

In Chapter 3, I identified some such characteristics with regard to the lesson plan. Davidson (1996, page.11-14) identifies six general criteria or characteristics of a 'good geography lesson' from her experience as an OFSTED inspector and tutor for geography education:

*   ***Learning objectives.*** *A good lesson has clear and appropriate learning objectives which are previewed and shared with the pupils drawing on their existing knowledge and experience.*
*   ***Differentiation.*** *In a good lesson pupils with differing abilities are able to make progress in learning, and tasks and activities are within the extended grasp of all pupils.*
*   ***Teaching and learning strategies.*** *In a good lesson a variety of strategies are used to create a range of learning opportunities suited to the needs of all pupils. The strategies provide opportunities to make progress and develop learning skills.*
*   ***Lesson structure.*** *A good lesson is well structured to maintain challenge, pace and motivation.*
*   ***Assessment.*** *In a good lesson assessment is integral and used to identify pupils' strengths and needs. Pupils are given formative feedback to help them develop and are encouraged to engage in self assessment.*
*   ***Evaluation.*** *In a good lesson the outcomes are reviewed with the pupils and used to inform teaching and learning.*

Activity - reviewing your teaching

1. Critically evaluate the above set of attributes for a good geography lesson. Are there any you would wish to reject, or modify? Are there any you would wish to add?
2. Apply the criteria to some of your own lessons (perhaps 3 or 4). You can do this alone, though obviously you are too busy to stand back from a lesson in progess and evaluate it 'on the spot'. Because of this you may well find it appropriate to enlist the assistance of someone else (eg mentor, tutor or peer partner) to assist you in this reviewing process by asking them to observe at least one lesson and give you feedback in the light of the criteria.

3.   Review your teaching in the light of what you learn. The aim of this is to enable you to identify an aspect which you feel could be improved.

Planning for development

In the light of the above review of teaching, formulate an **action plan** to build on what you now know about your teaching. This might include the following stages:

- *set a specific target for development (you may find it helpful to do this through discussion, eg with a mentor);*
- *plan a timeline for investigating your chosen issue, acting on the findings and evaluating progress;*
- *collect more data about your own teaching if necessary;*
- *find out more about your chosen area of interest, eg through reading and discussion with colleagues;*
- *arrange to conduct some observations of your own, focusing on your chosen aspect (you may find it helpful to discuss this with your mentor or professional tutor first);*
- *review and reflect on what you have learned;*
- *systematically incorporate the results into your own teaching;*
- *evaluate the extent to which the target for development has been achieved.*

Note

The process described above of self-review leading to action planning, implementation and evaluation links with wider processes of review and planning for development. This is true at the individual level, through processes of induction and appraisal, at the team/group level (key stage/subject/department/year) and at the whole school level.

5

Resources and approaches for learning

"To see a World in a grain of sand,
And a Heaven in a wild flower..."

William Blake

Aims

This Chapter seeks to focus more closely on the resources for learning which you will use in your teaching of geography. It also focuses on some of the many approaches to learning which should be central to your 'repertoire' as a teacher of geography:

* *the development of a sense of place;*
* *the use of fieldwork;*
* *the use of information technology;*
* *active learning;*
* *the development of graphicacy.*

The intention is that you will systematically make use of these possibilities where appropriate, thereby enhancing both your provision of learning opportunities for those whom you teach, and your ongoing process of professional development in teaching.

Resources for teaching and learning

When it comes to resources for teaching and learning in geography, the world really is our oyster! Wherever possible we will want to study that world at first hand. Bringing the world into the classroom can only really be second best. But of course there are numerous constraints (finance, time, distance, complexity, safety etc) which mean that very often we will set up learning experiences in the classroom. In our thinking about resources, then, we should start with the world itself, simultaneously both the object of study and a resource for teaching and learning in its own right.

Palmer (1994, p.168) makes the point that "successful teaching and learning in geography are inevitably dependent to a greater or lesser extent on resources. The creative teacher, she indicates, will always be consciously on the look-out for low cost, appropriate resources. In **Beginning Teaching Workbook 2** (Tolley et al, 1996, p.28) we suggested that "just about anything you can think of" could be a resource for teaching and learning. Powell (1991, p.12) comments that "defining resources, therefore, is simple. *If you can make use of it, it is a resource!*"

Thus the identification of resources is closely associated with the identification of objectives in the form of intended learning outcomes and with the choice of methodology to achieve those outcomes, as shown in **Figure 5.1**.

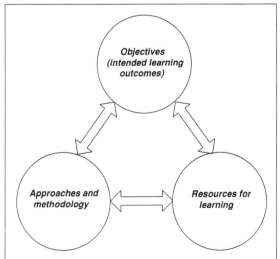

Figure 5.1 The relationship between resources, objectives and methodology.

Normally the objectives will be set first, occupying a primary position in the three-way relationship pictured. However, many teachers have had the experience of finding an attractive potential resource and looking for a context in which to use it. Also, availability of resources and practicability of approaches may have a modifying effect on the objectives as set, so the situation is more dynamic and two-way than a strictly 'objectives-led' approach might suggest.

Geography as a resource

Derricott (1994, pages 9 - 22) suggests that geography itself, along with other subjects, can be seen as "a resource for teachers to use in approaching their curriculum planning and in developing appropriate, related teaching and learning experiences". He suggests that as a distinctive subject resource, geography can offer young people:

- *relevance to their own lives, including opportunities to investigate the key concepts of similarity and difference;*
- *realistic situations in which to explore issues involving values;*
- *opportunities to engage in critical thinking, the collection and evaluation of evidence and the exercise of empathy;*
- *opportunities to develop the capability of thinking spatially in terms of distributions, processes and outcomes;*
- *the opportunity to develop a global perspective by relating the local to the global, through working across a range of scales.*

In so doing he draws on the work of the Schools' Council *Place, Time and Society* Project. Though the target age group for the project was 8 - 13 (the 'Middle Schools' age range, covering much of key stages 2 and 3) it is possible to project these contributions of geography as a resource into other age groups.

Activity

1. Critically consider the list of bullet points (above).
2. To what extent do you agree that they represent the distinctive contribution which geography can make to young people's learning? (You may wish to amend or add to the list)
3. To what extent would you say your teaching emphasises these distinctive contributions of geography? What evidence can you use to support your answer?

Resources for geography

In the previous section, 'Geography as a resource', we considered the distinctive contribution that geography can make to the nature of learning experiences. This is important in setting up contexts for learning in geography, but of course our search for resources does not stop there. Below is a check list of some types of resources for teaching and learning in geography. Though it is extensive, because of the nature of geography the list cannot be exhaustive. However, it does offer some in pointers for your thinking about the resources you may wish to use in your planning and teaching.

• **The learners themselves:**	*their prior knowledge and experience, including hobbies and interests*
	their imaginations
• **Yourself:**	*your knowledge and experience*
	your possessions, eg holiday souvenirs
• **Your teaching colleagues:**	*their knowledge and experience, including alternative perspectives and ideas*
• **Adults other than teachers (AOTs):**	*parents and other members of the local community with different jobs, countries of origin etc*
	your non-teaching colleagues (eg secretary, caretaker) and the school's governors
	local residents with particular views, interests, memories

| | | contacts in other fields, eg planning department, archives office, local media, local weather station, farming |
| | | contacts in the voluntary sector, eg charities, conservation |

- **The classroom:**   its facilities (chalkboard, 'dry wipe' board, noticeboards, display space, flip-chart, overhead projector, tables etc.)

  its shape, dimensions and subdivisions

- **The school:**   its buildings (including other rooms and their functions, external features etc.)

  its library and other collections

  its grounds (vegetation, soil, ground cover, slope, aspect, playground markings)

  its behavioural character (routes, busy and quiet areas, hazards and safe areas etc.)

  its environmental quality

  The school grounds as a resource Palmer (1994, pages 78 - 84) describes the use of a school's grounds in providing for early years geography.

- **The world beyond the school:**   the view through the window and from the school grounds

  the local area in walking distance, including its land use (parks, shops, streets, housing, derelict land, agriculture, transport, industry) and physical features (hills, valleys, rivers etc.), its behavioural character and environmental quality

  locations for fieldwork and visits (museums, nature reserves, factories, public and religious buildings, study centres (urban/field)

- **Printed material:**   published and/or 'home produced'

  books (textbooks, reference, fiction)

  worksheets and information sheets

  newspapers and magazines

  cartoons and drawings

  photographs, aerial photographs and remote-sensing images

  posters and wall charts

  maps and atlases

  graphs, charts and statistical diagrams

  leaflets, brochures and other documents

  Fiction and geography at KS1 and 2 Palmer (pages 171 - 174) provides a lengthy list of story books which can provide starting points for early years geography. Krause (1994, pages 136 -155) provides an exploration of the use of literature in geography in the primary school, together with some suggested titles. Other suggestions are listed in NICED (1988, pages 51 - 53).

- **Audio-visual:**   live broadcasts on radio and TV

  video tapes

  audio tapes (speech, music, sound effects)

  slides and filmstrips

  camera and video camera

- **Information technology:**   hardware: computers, printers, concept keyboard, CD ROM drive, scanner, sensors, probes and other data gathering equipment (eg automatic weather station, satellite receiving/decoding equipment), turtle, digital camera, fax machine, modem, calculator

  software: programs (wordprocessor, database, graphing, spreadsheet, simulations, geographic information system, e-mail, web browser), CD ROMs, datafiles, text files and clip art

- **Other equipment:**   soil testing kit, soil auger, infiltrometer, pH meter

  compasses, measuring tapes, clinometer

  thermometers, rain gauge, barometer, anemometer, light meter, Stevenson screen

	clipboards, stopwatches
	rulers, protractors, compasses, stencils, templates, scissors, stapler, hole punch, trigger tacker
• **Consumables:**	paper (plain, lined, squared), card, backing paper, files, exercise books
	map outlines
	pens, pencils, crayons, markers
	glue, staples, 'blutak', display pins
• **Models:**	scale models, landscape models, cross-sections and cutaways, globes etc.
• **Objects:**	specimens, eg pebbles, rocks and fossils
	artefacts, eg clothing, craft objects, domestic equipment, musical instruments
	'realia' to help give a feel for distant places, eg tickets, menus, labels and packaging, postcards and stamps, till receipts, programmes and guides, posters and notices
• **Food and drink:**	dishes to taste and smell, including 'typical' dishes and special/celebratory dishes
	fruit, vegetables, herbs, spices and other ingredients
• **Games and activities:**	board games with a geographical dimension
	geographical word games
	games involving grids and coordinates
	orienteering and other outdoor pursuits

It is unlikely that any one teacher of geography will use all the items in this list, though some may well get close! My purpose in including it here is for you to use it as:

- *a sort of 'idea jogger' and aid to your planning (- a resource in its own right!);*
- *a checklist for auditing your use of resources in your teaching;*
- *an inventory for investigating what is available.*

Action point
Have you conducted a thorough resources audit in the school/department in which you are currently working, and filed the results with your lesson plans?

Selecting resources

As noted above in **Figure 5.1**, the selection of resources is closely bound up with the learning objectives and the choice of methodology. It is important in your selection of any resource that you remember to evaluate it carefully before using it. You should as a minimum consider the following:

- ***Fitness for purpose:*** *is the resource appropriate for the learning purpose/s for which you are considering it? Does it support an enquiry approach? Is it better than any alternatives?*
- ***Practicability:*** *is it feasible to use the resource/s in the manner envisaged? Will any special facilities, arrangements or adaptations be needed? Are there any health and safety implications?*
- ***Availability:*** *is the resource available when needed? Do you know where it is kept? Does it need to be booked in advance, or other arrangements made?*
- ***Bias and stereotypes:*** *how are men and women presented? How are different cultures presented? Do the resources support good practice in multicultural education, and in education for equal opportunities?*
- ***Cost:*** *if the resource is to be bought, hired or consumed, what are the financial implications?*
- ***Access:*** *does it provide or support learning opportunities for **all** the intended users in ways appropriate to their individual needs?*

In Beginning Teaching Workbook 3 (Tolley et al, pages 6-7) we suggest that a resources audit is an important component of your orientation in new teaching circumstances, eg at the start of a teaching practice, or when starting a new appointment, whether as an NQT or a more experienced teacher. We all need to know where things are!

In Beginning Teaching Workbook 2 (Tolley et al, op cit, p.29) we provide a resource evaluation schedule, together with other comments on using and developing resources (pages 28 to 34)

Wiegand (1992, pages 96 - 126) deals in some detail with the presentation of distant places and people in fiction and non fiction, and in particular issues of racism and ethnocentrism.

1. Consider a sequence of lessons you have taught recently or are about to teach. Critically evaluate the sequence from the point of view of resource usage. Did you/will you use a variety of resources? Are there opportunities for you to think more creatively about your choice and use of resources?
2. Focus on the resources actually in use in your lessons. How do they measure up against the six criteria listed above?

Approaches to teaching geography (i) - a sense of place

> *"Fragmentation of knowledge, social differentiation and the questioning of scientific rationality have all coalesced to reaffirm the importance of the particular, the specific, the local. And in this social and cognitive environment a geography stressing the salience of place has great potential."*

> *Livingstone, 1997, p. 358*

I have already stressed the use of an enquiry approach to geographical study in Chapter 3. If you have not read that section yet, you should do so now. One of the purposes and consequences of using the enquiry approach is the development of a sense of place. The development of a sense of place was identified as one of the particular aims for geography in the National Curriculum (DES/WO, 1990, p.7), with the clarification that it involves "a feeling for the 'personality' of a place and what it might be like to live there".

Thus the sense of place emerges from the interaction of

The list of questions on page 22 show how an enquiry approach can be used in the development of a sense of place.

*   *knowledge about a place;*
*   *the individual's own attitudes and values;*
*   *a questioning, investigative approach.*

This interaction is represented diagramatically in **Figure 5.2.**

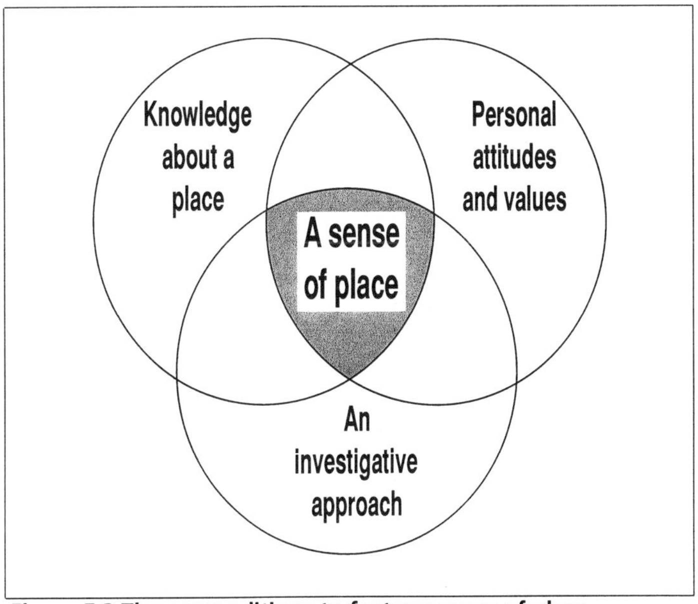

Figure 5.2 The preconditions to foster a sense of place

How can you approach your teaching is such a way as to foster this sense of place? Probably the best way is at first hand, through fieldwork (see next Section). Of course it is not possible to go to all the distant places we would wish to 'visit' in our teaching and learning about geography. However, it is important to provide a basis by fostering the sense of place through immediate experience where possible, initially in a familiar context. Thus, work investigating the classroom, the school and its grounds, and the neighbourhood in such a way as to clarify what they are like is of value. It gives each individual the opportunity to develop skills and examine her/his attitudes and values (eg "what I like and don't like about this place, and why," and "how it feels to be in this place and why"). Thus a critical perspective is brought to bear on an individual's sense of familiar places, fostering an awareness of the interaction between the individual's attitudes and values and her/his knowledge and perceptions of the place.

This then provides the basis for dealing with less familiar places in a similar way. However, instead of experiencing such places at first hand the 'experience' is a mixture of what, if anything, the students already know about such places, together with knowledge acquired through the learning activities and resources chosen by the teacher. The role of the teacher's planning is crucial here.

Wiegand (1992, p.31) identifies two distinct approaches to teaching about distant places. The first involves setting out to "predispose children to think positively about other places and people" by carefully selecting the resources and stimuli which are to be used, and attempting to manage the responses towards desired outcomes. The other approach involves opening up and examining the process whereby places come to be 'known' and through which attitudes towards them are developed and expressed.

The work based in the immediate locality, described above, is of the second type. Much work can be a mixture of both types. The study of a place can begin with the question "What do we already know about place X?" The question can be put directly, or the image of a place can be investigated by using a 'trigger', eg "Write down five words that you think of when I say...... 'Eskimo'." Potentially this can generate 150 different words from a class of 30. In practice there are overlaps and clusters, eg igloo, cold, seal, snow, North Pole etc. The individual associations are pooled to tease out the 'group image', eg 21 people wrote 'igloo', 17 wrote 'cold', 15 'snow' etc. This image can then be examined, eg "Why did so many people write down these things?" "Has anyone been to where the 'Eskimo' live?" "Does anyone know any 'Eskimo' people?" "Where has our image come from?" "Is it accurate? How do we know?" This represents the second approach given above, and can be done for any location given an appropriate trigger.

In this example, the teacher went on to introduce the idea of names, including our personal names and how we prefer them to be used. The information was then introduced that a number of the groups generally referred to as 'Eskimo' actually call themselves 'Inuit', which means 'the people' in Inuutituk. The word 'Eskimo' is possibly derived from 'eskipot', an Algonquin word meaning 'eater of raw flesh', which might be seen as derogatory; it is also an outsider's description. Unsurprisingly the class felt that it would be more appropriate to refer to these people as Inuit from that point on. This is more in line with Wiegand's first type of approach. Video extracts and photographs were then used to develop a sense of place and empathy with the lives of the Inuit.

Hughes and Marsden (1994, pages 50 - 61) describe their approach to developing and resourcing a study of Blanes as a distant locality at greater length, giving more detail about aspects of the geography and the resources they gathered.

In their preparation of work investigating a European locality, Hughes and Marsden (1994, p. 51) decided that "though it may not be practical to take a whole class of children abroad, a distant place study obviously gains if the teacher has had firsthand experience of it." They therefore visited the chosen locality, Blanes on the Costa Brava in Spain, to research the locality, take photographs and acquire resources. This they felt would lead to a more authentic portrayal of Blanes back in the classroom, with greater potential for fostering a sense of place and avoiding problems of superficiality and stereotyping.

Wiegand (p.34) acknowledges the complexity of achieving a sense of place in the classroom. It involves:

- *developing an accurate framework of locational knowledge (ie, where places are);*
- *providing, as far as possible, accurate mental images of the nature of other places;*
- *fostering positive attitudes towards distinctive aspects of other places and ways of life.*

We can see that the goal of developing a sense of place in those whom you teach is far from simple. If you are to do it effectively you will need to draw on a range of professional skills and understandings in choosing the ingredients and putting them together. In your planning you will choose places from around the world at a range of scales and degrees of unfamiliarity. Your choice will be influenced by your access to resources and your ability to foster a sense of place.

> "When I taught geography I was sometimes guilty of presenting places as examples of, say particular arrangements of land use or industrial activity. With inadequate visual material and no time spent on attempting to build the 'personality' of a place (good geography teachers use travellers' tales, literature, music....) regional studies became sterile lists. For many pupils Dundee is 'jute, jam and journalism'. No more than that."
>
> Wiegand, p.33

A Level and A/S Level students too are required to study a chosen 'physical environment' and a chosen 'human environment', giving new emphasis to the study of real places in the post-16 curriculum.

Through experience you will come to recognise the resources and approaches which seem to work best when you set out to bring the world into your classroom; where possible you will also use an authentic voice - your own, one of the children's, a visitor's - to be the catalyst which enables the interaction between knowledge and attitudes to yield a true sense of place.

Activity

1. Review your teaching about places. How much of it fits Wiegand's description (above)?
2. Develop a learning activity which particularly sets out to develop a sense of place, to be used with a class you teach.
3. Decide on the resources you are going to use. You may want to refer back to the resources list for some ideas. Remember that your choice of resources should support the development of a sense of place.
4. How are you going to evaluate the effectiveness of your activity in developing a sense of place? (This may be something to discuss with a colleague who knows geography, your mentor or your HE Tutor, as appropriate)

Approaches to teaching geography (ii) - Fieldwork

For some, the word 'fieldwork' conjures up a picture of dejected students with sodden anoraks and soggy notebooks huddled together halfway up a wet and windy hillside. Whilst this is indeed an image of some fieldwork, it is rather limited. What about the survey of busy and quiet areas around the school, or the visit to the local light industrial estate? It may be better to think of fieldwork as 'work outside the classroom' (though this too is limited in that some fieldwork techniques, eg measuring, taking bearings, conducting questionnaire surveys etc can of course be practised inside the classroom if necessary!).

Fieldwork, as noted in the previous section, has much to contribute to the development of an individual's sense of place. Other benefits or advantages of fieldwork are:

- *it emphasises that geography is the study of real places;*
- *it provides a basis for learning about more distant places;*
- *it provides a context for developing an enquiry approach;*
- *it brings enhanced meaning and clarification to ideas and terminology used in the classroom;*
- *it provides an excellent context for the development of a wide range of skills, from observation and recording to social and teamwork skills;*
- *it often has an observably beneficial impact on interest and motivation;*
- *it provides an opportunity for the exercise of autonomy and 'self-managed learning';*
- *it provides a context for other learning, eg environmental education;*
- *it provides a basis for work back in school;*
- *it encourages the use of language;*
- *it provides a context for different types of investigation, from quantitative survey to sensory impressions.*

It is important not to think of fieldwork as a one-off activity: it needs a clearly established context. It can, of course, be used as a high-profile introduction to a topic, or as a follow-up to work undertaken in the classroom. At other times there will be both preparation and follow-up, both taking place in the classroom, in order to maximise the benefit of the time spent investigating 'in the field', as shown in **Figure 5.3**.

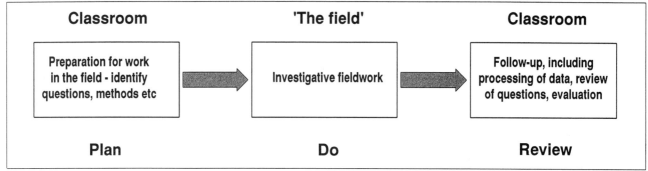

Figure 5.3 A three stage approach to fieldwork

The diagram (**Figure 5.3**) stresses an enquiry approach involving investigative fieldwork. Note too that it has clear parallels with the plan-do-review model with which you are familiar. It is an opportunity to introduce your students to this way of thinking about their work. As with any enquiry-based approach, there will be decisions to be made about the balance between autonomy and teacher-direction (see Chapter 3). There is of course also an opportunity for field **teaching** (as distinct from field**work**); again you will have to decide on what is an appropriate balance in the circumstances in which you are working.

A questioning approach is important, and the nature of the questions will have an impact on the manner in which the data will be collected. You will have to decide whether you or the students are going to make the decisions about the appropriate methods of data collection. Such data collection can involve one or more of:

- *sensory experience and impressions, eg sounds, visual impact, smells;*
- *counting, eg pedestrian count, traffic census, building storeys;*
- *measuring, eg dimensions of a stream channel, infiltration rate, windspeed;*
- *interviews and questionnaires, eg a survey of shoppers;*
- *sampling, eg quadrat, transect;*
- *direct observation, eg cloud types, land uses;*
- *taking of photographs, eg with a polaroid camera or a digital camera;*
- *drawing of field sketches and sketch maps;*
- *using portable tape-recorders, eg to record own impressions or interviews with others;*
- *using portable video cameras;*
- *writing in notebooks or on prepared maps, recording grids and schedules;*
- *using portable computers (palmtops and laptops);*
- *using probes and datalogging equipment;*
- *collecting samples, eg pebbles, soil samples.*

Fieldwork

Your school's policy regarding outdoor activities should reflect the safety requirement of legislation introduced in 1996. Check that it is accurate and up-to-date.

Action point

Your school should have a policy for any 'off-site' activity involving children. Ensure that you are fully acquainted with the policy and any associated procedures before planning any fieldwork. (Remember that you can use the school and its grounds for fieldwork without having to make special arrangements.)

Activity

The planning and carrying out of fieldwork is a major professional development activity. You are strongly advised to do this, both as an enhancement of your geography teaching and as a vehicle for your ongoing professional development. **Note that you should consult with your mentor / head of department / professional tutor before undertaking this activity.**

1. Identify a curriculum opportunity for fieldwork, and identify an appropriate site or venue.
2. Produce a planning time line in the light of the school's policy and procedures, identifying key dates in the run-up to your proposed fieldwork.
3. Undertake preliminary, preparatory work by visiting the site, checking on access, opening times etc as appropriate.

4. Evaluate the site for any health and safety considerations.
5. Identify any necessary amenities, eg toilets, places to eat lunch, shelter etc as appropriate.
6. Produce a draft plan for the fieldwork, including the aims and objectives, timings, main activities etc. Seek approval as appropriate.
7. If the participants have to miss lessons with other teachers, seek their agreement.
8. Plan for the evaluation of the fieldwork: what are your evaluation criteria?
9. Make arrangements for transport, if needed.
10. Make arrangements for appropriate staffing, bearing in mind supervision ratio for off-site work etc. (This will normally be done in consultation with a senior member of staff)
11. Make contingency plans for adverse weather conditions.
12. Plan and produce any necessary materials, eg base maps.
13. Notify parents in writing about the fieldwork, including information about the site and programme, date and timings, eating arrangements, any particular clothing requirements and any cost. (This letter will normally be drafted in consultation with your mentor / head of department. Note that charges can only be made under the provisions of the school's agreed charging policy) You may also wish to offer parents the opportunity to participate. Your letter will also seek their formal consent to their child's participation (the school will have a proforma for this) and information about any medical concerns (eg asthma, diabetes) and emergency contact arrangements.
14. Carry out any necessary preliminary teaching.
15. Collect necessary payment, recording all monies collected according to school procedures.
16. Collect and file all consent forms.
17. If you have teaching which is being 'covered' by other colleagues, ensure that any necessary work is set.
18. Conduct final check of all arrangements.
19. The above may sound like a lot of work. It is! Nevertheless, fieldwork is normally very enjoyable for all involved, and of enormous value as a learning experience, so **enjoy your field trip!**
20. Carry out follow-up as appropriate.
21. Evaluate the fieldwork according to the criteria you have identified.
22. Make an appropriate entry in your reflective journal. Try to comment on how you have benefited in terms of your professional development.

Fieldwork- Your legal position
- *The school's governors are required by law to satisfy themselves of the adequacy of your plans for the safe conduct of any visits out of school. This is reflected in the school's policy and procedures.*
- *Most of the teachers' Unions offer advice to their members in the form of leaflets regarding visits out of school. You are advised to consult these.*
- *It cannot be stressed too strongly that it is vital for your own protection and that of the young people in your care that you take full and careful account of any guidelines, and follow any requirements 'to the letter'.*

Collecting money
It is important that you follow correct procedures, again for your own protection. All individual payments must be recorded and monies 'banked' with the school secretary as having been officially received. Under no circumstances use the cash yourself.

Approaches to teaching geography (iii) - Using new technologies

"The enormous potential of IT (information technology) to change the focus of education from teaching to learning can be compared with the spread of literacy which resulted from the printing press."

Davis, 1992

In a remarkably short time information technology has become part and parcel of the educational scene. Elsewhere (Fisher, 1996) I have noted that:

- *It is seen as a subject in its own right with its own set of statutory orders in the National Curriculum.*
- *It is a 'Common Requirement' of all National Curriculum Programmes of Study for England and Wales which states that "pupils should be given opportunities, where appropriate, to develop and apply their information technology (IT) capability in their study of the subjects (PE is exempted from this requirement)." (SCAA/ACAC, 1996, p.6)*
- *It is recognised as a 'cross-curricular skill' alongside literacy, numeracy, study, personal/social skills and problem-solving (eg, NCC, 1989).*
- *It is used as a resource to support learning in a range of subjects and topics.*
- *It seems to be widely recognised as being beneficial to motivation in a variety of contexts.*
- *It has enabled enhanced provision to be made for those identified as having certain 'special educational needs'.*
- *It is increasingly a capability which children bring to their educational experience, via the expanding home market for personal computing and multimedia 'edutainment' systems.*

Using IT in your teaching of geography

It is beyond the aims and scope of this book to go into detail about the ways in which you can use IT to support teaching and learning in geography. My concern here is that you should actively use IT as an aspect of your professional development as a teacher of geography.

Further guidance about the use of IT to support teaching and learning in geography can be found in:

- *Martin, F (1996)* **Teaching Early Years Geography** *(pages 39 - 48);*
- *Chambers, B and Donert, K (1996)* **Teaching Geography at Key Stage 2** *(pages 44 to 56);*
- *Battersby , J (1996)* **Teaching Geography at Key Stage 3** *(pages 17 - 20):*
- *GA/NCET (1994ª) Gegraphy: a pupil's entitlement for IT;*
- *GA/NCET (1995ª) Primary geography: a pupil's entitlement for IT ;*
- *Kent, A and Phillips, A (1994) 'Geography through Information Technology: Supporting Geographical Enquiry' in Marsden and Hughes,* **Primary School Geography;**
- *GA/NCET (1995ᵇ)* **Using IT to enhance geography: case studies at key stages 3 and 4;**
- *GA/NCET (1995ᶜ)* **Investigating Weather Data - a resource booklet for teachers**
- *GA/NCET (1994ᵇ)* **Shopping and Traffic Fieldwork - a resource booklet for teachers**
- *NCET (1995)* **Approaches to IT capability**
- *Regular features on geography and IT appear in* **Primary Geographer** *and* **Teaching Geography,** *both published by the GA.*

- *It gives access to increased and enhanced information sources for learning (CD ROM, E-mail, Campus 2000, the World-Wide Web).*
- *Some teachers are finding that IT supports them in other aspects of their work, eg production of resources, keeping of records, writing of reports.*

How many of these intersect, either actually or potentially, with your work as a teacher of geography? Probably all of them! **Figure 5.4** summarises some aspects of the relationship.

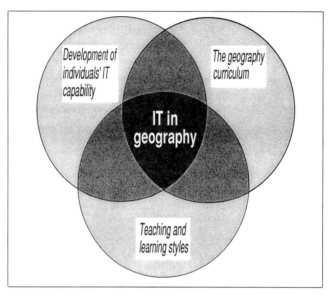

Figure 5.4 Some aspects of IT in geography

In the publication *Geography: a pupil's entitlement for IT* the following were proposed as the reasons why young people should be enabled to use IT in geography:

- *"to enhance their skills of geographical enquiry;*
- *to gain access to a wide range of geographical knowledge and information sources;*
- *to deepen their understanding of environmental and spatial relationships;*
- *to experience alternative images of people, place and environment;*
- *to consider the wider impact of IT on people, place and environment."*

(GA/NCET, 1994ª, 1995ª)

IT can enrich the quality of learning in geography in the following ways. It can:

- *"extend knowledge and understanding by providing images and information not otherwise readily available;*
- *enhance the enquiry process through access to in-depth data;*
- *provide the capability to look for patterns and relationships by manipulating large data sets;*
- *increase the time for greater depth of analysis, by generating graphs, charts and maps rapidly;*
- *support analytical thinking and problem-solving through the design and refinement of simple models;*
- *develop graphicacy skills;*
- *try different types of graphs and consider which is appropriate and most informative;*
- *facilitate the communication of geographical ideas by enabling pupils to integrate text, graphs and images into high-quality reports;*
- *provide more accurate and consistent data than would otherwise be possible;*
- *motivate pupils, providing new challenges and experiences;*
- *act as a focus for exploration of ideas, encouraging discussion and reflection;*
- *encourage pupils to develop an increased autonomy in their learning."*

(GA/NCET, 1995ᵇ, pages.8-9)

Activity (1)

1. Read the following two extracts:

   ### Extract 1

   "Some call the effects of microcomputers on schools a revolution. Revolution may seem a strong word to describe the advent of 'educational computing'. It isn't. Nothing before has so stirred schools into action. School systems, teachers, parents and children talk about computers as they never talked about programmed learning, educational television, open education nor raising the school leaving age, for that matter. Schools must have computers! People talk about how children are captivated by computer assisted learning (CAL) while others stress computer-based jobs. Yet others urge affirmative action and remediation through CAL. Others point to the demands of a technological culture when urging schools to use computers. On a different track some see a potential for more and better social and intellectual activities in schools. Others stress self-image and self-expression. The range of possibilities is exceptional. No other educational technology has been thought to have such potential." (Olson, 1988, p.1)

   ### Extract 2

   "In recent times, solutions to pedagogical problems have very often been sought by the use of various types of technology. Enthusiasm for aids such as language laboratories, teaching machines, closed circuit TV and currently, computers, videodisks, lasers, multimedia 'presentations' have promised the pedagogical holy grail. In due course some of them have been absorbed into the teacher's armamentarium, others gather dust in stock rooms. None has brought the prophesied pedagogical millennium." (Stones, 1992 p.8)

2. How do you explain the rather different positions adopted by the two authors?
3. Which of the two extracts is nearest to your own position on the likely impact of IT in schools?

Activity (2)

1. If you have not yet done so, carry out a resources audit for IT in your school. Note the hardware and software which are available, and any access conditions (booking arrangements, licence conditions etc.)
2. Carry out a 'force-field analysis' of the factors influencing the further development of your use of IT in your teaching. Use a frame like the one in **Figure 5.5** to classify factors (eg, access to hardware, department policy, network facilities etc) into restraining forces (holding back the innovation) and driving forces (which are propelling it forward).

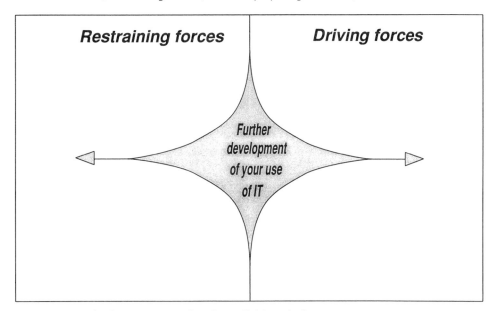

The technique of force field analysis is similar to SWOT analysis which we considered earlier; indeed, it is sometimes preceded by a SWOT analysis. Both techniques have a similar purpose: to assist in the analysis of a situation and help in the process of making soundly-based decisions about what to do next.

Figure 5.5 Developing your use of IT: force field analysis

3. Action plan the next stage of your professional development in the use of IT, in the light of your force field analysis. This will involve minimising the restraining forces and maximising any forces which are driving the innovation forward. (This would be a good focus for a professional discussion with your mentor / professional tutor / head of department. If you are a student teacher, it might be possible to spend some time working with a colleague or visiting another school to observe and discuss aspects of IT in use. If you are already working as a teacher, clearly the same is possible, but you may also have access to some courses via the school's staff development arragements. You may even feel that it would be good for your development to run some in-service training for colleagues who are less confident and/or competent in the use of IT.

Approaches to teaching geography (iv) - Active learning

"Active learning refers to any activities where pupils are given a marked degree of autonomy and control over the organisation, conduct and direction of the learning activity." (Kyriacou, 1991, p.42) However, as Kyriacou goes on to note, active learning is somewhat ill-defined, and is used to refer to many different approaches to teaching and learning. It is probably safe to say that 'doing', as opposed to sitting and listening, lies at the heart of active learning, though it is important to remember that there are many types of 'doing', not all of which involve getting into groups, getting out of one's place or making a noise and/or a mess!

Many of the comments made elsewhere in this book about teaching and learning in geography point strongly in the direction of active learning, eg fieldwork and enquiry. Indeed, the approach to professional development which underlies this book is one which acknowledges that a significant part of your professional learning about teaching will be gained through active methods (teaching, going and finding out, discussion), which in turn require **you** to function autonomously in your learning.

At the time of writing there is a public debate about teaching methods and their effectiveness. In some of its less well-informed manifestations, the debate sets active learning methods in false opposition to whole class 'didactic' teaching. It is of course perfectly possible to have both if the test of 'fitness for purpose' is applied. If young people are to develop flexibility, cooperation, team-working and other inter-personal skills, and the autonomy to learn new skills and competences to keep pace with the knowledge explosion and social and technological change, then approaches involving active learning not only have a place: they are essential.

Active learning, as indicated above, seeks to foster autonomy. Nolen (1995) notes that there are three types of autonomy. The development of autonomy among learners is not just about **autonomy of means** (some choices about how to do something, eg design a poster or write a poem) or even **autonomy of purpose** (ie, intrinsic as opposed to extrinsic motivation: 'do it for yourself, not just because I say so'). The greatest is **intellectual (and moral) autonomy** (p.202) which is the ability to judge things for oneself taking account of evidence and views. Students who have intellectual autonomy therefore evaluate their own work and that of others. They critcally evaluate arguments. Those with moral autonomy recognise the difference between right and wrong, regardless of rewards or punishments, taking account of - but not necessarily following - the views of others.

As an approach active learning is somewhat analogous to the 'open' question, in that the parameters for the response are not narrowly set. Instead, many active learning situations have a quality of open-endedness which enable learners to come up with their own meanings, procedures, interpretations, or results. However, it is vital that this take place within a framework of clearly articulated objectives as intended learning outcomes. (see also Chapter 4) Active learning must be purposeful and be seen to be 'going somewhere'.

Active learning can take a number of forms. Some examples are:

*   *Individual research or project*, eg journey to work patterns of neighbours;
*   *Group research or project* with division of responsibilities, eg different aspects of flood hazard;

"What we have to learn to do, we learn by doing." (Aristotle)

- **Whole class role play**, eg a planning inquiry with presentations from different interest groups;
- **Small group drama**, eg improvised family discussion about where to go on holiday;
- **Locational decision-making simulation**, eg where to site a new airport;
- **Process simulation,** eg the development of a transport network;
- **Games**, eg a farming game, which simulates crop decisions and their consequences;
- **Small group discussion**, eg predicting what will happen next in a paused video, and justifying the prediction.

Some active learning approaches require several hours of work, eg individual or group research projects leading to presentations. Others may take only a few minutes, eg, during study of, say, land use conflict in National Parks, each member of class jots down three questions they would want to ask a park warden for a TV documentary. Then, in pairs, they role play the questions and answers.

Bale (1987, p.125) identifies four main purposes underlying the use of those active learning approaches we could group together as 'simulations'. They are:

- **the development of empathy** with people from other places, living in other circumstances and environments;
- **improved understanding of working processes**, eg decision making processes:
- **recognition of 'interdisciplinary' nature of real life situations;**
- **improved levels of motivation.**

> *Empathy means the ability to identify with someone else's situation or circumstances. It does not mean accepting their point of view uncritically.*

Steiner (1996, p. 199) notes that there is "a large body of research (which) supports both the social and the cognitive gains children can make through participating in structured collaborative and co-operative activities." One of the reasons for these gains is that children do not acquire learning in one single act of understanding. Rather, meaning is *constructed* through a continuous process involving the constant testing and reformulation of the child's ideas. This is best supported in a social, collaborative environment, and this in turn stimulates and supports talk, which is an important aspect of active learning approaches.

> *Constructivism*
> *The approach to learning described here is referred to as the **constructivist** approach. It owes much to the work of the psychologist Lev Vygotsky. Vygotsky identifies those things which are not quite within the learner's independent grasp as lying within that individual's 'zone of proximal development'. He/she can be assisted to do these things through co-operation with more knowledgeable others, who may be fellow learners, but also teachers, other adults etc. (See, for instance, Bennett and Dunne, 1994, p.50 ff)*

An equally important aspect of active learning is that there should be some form of debriefing at the end. Through such a debriefing your aim will be to clarify and consolidate the learning which has occurred through an evaluation of what has taken place. The debriefing may involve further active approaches, (eg group discussion around the question "What have we learnt from this activity?") or individual reflection and written comment (eg "Three things I learnt from this activity were.....").

Overall the point which is being made in this section is that active learning approaches are a vital part of the geography teacher's methodological repertoire, but they are far from being a soft option! They have to be very carefully planned and set up, well managed and concluded effectively. If not they are quite likely to yield either relatively undemanding 'busy work' or unproductive off-task activity, in both of which little true learning takes place.

Activity

> *Observing active learning*
> *You may find it useful to observe either within the subject area of geography or to look at something within a completely different subject context (or both, if circumstances permit).*

1. Review your own teaching for your use of active learning approaches. Are you using them enough / too much? How well are you using them? How do you know?
2. Observe a colleague teaching a lesson in which an active approach is emphasised. Take particular note of the following:
   - the teacher's planning and preparation, including objectives of the activity;
   - how the teacher sets up the activity;
   - how the activity is managed;
   - how the activity is debriefed.
3. A second observation possibility (ideally you will do both) is to do an in-depth but discreet observation of a chosen student during a lesson involving an active learning approach:
   - what does he/she do during the 'setting up' phase?
   - during the activity, how much time is spent on and off-task?;
   - how many times does he/she speak, to whom, and on whose initiative?;
   - what does he/she do during the debriefing?

4. Set up a lesson in which you are emphasising an active learning approach. Ask your mentor or another colleague to observe your management of the lesson and the learners' responses. Discuss the feedback with the observer.
5. Review the results of these observations, perhaps by means of discussion with a colleague.
6. Identify targets for development in your use of active learning approaches.

Approaches to teaching geography (v) - developing graphicacy

Graphicacy can be thought of as the condition of being able to communicate and interpret graphical and visual information incorporating a spatial component (ie 'the world from above' at varying degrees of abstraction). Clearly this is important in geography for it is often not possible to study the world at first hand: it is necessary therefore to represent it in some way, in the classroom. This representation emphasises the use of maps, but also includes aerial photographs and remote-sensed images, and diagrams of various kinds.

As with numeracy, literacy and oracy, graphicacy is not a 'steady-state condition'. That is to say, it is an improvable collection of separate sub-skills which are developed through on-going processes. For example, in the case of literacy we are familiar with the idea of an individual's 'reading age', and how the aim of teaching someone to read is fulfilled through a process extending over a number of years. The development of graphicacy is similar, though we do not go as far as identifying a map-reading age! This is because, though advanced map reading requires the simultaneous exercise of a number of cognitive skills and the wielding of several concepts, there is no particular order in which those skills and concepts are to be acquired beyond certain rules of thumb, such as not trying to do detailed work with contour lines before, say, scale and symbolisation have been grasped, or not trying to use Ordnance Survey maps before simple plans have been encountered.

Progression in graphicacy in the National Curriculum. (All are from Section 3, developing geographical skills)		
Key Stage 1 POS	Key Stage 2 POS	Key Stage 3 POS
"make maps and plans of real and imaginary places using pictures and symbols, *eg a pictorial map of a place featured in a story, a plan of their route from home to school*"	"make plans and maps at a variety of scales, using symbols and keys, *eg drawing a sketch map of a housing estate*"	"make maps and plans at a variety of scales, using symbols, keys and scales, *eg an annotated sketch map showing key features drawn from an OS map*"
"use globes, maps and plans at a variety of scales; the work should include identifying major geographical features.... locating and naming on a map the constituent countries of the United Kingdom, marking on a map approximately where they live, and following a route"	"use and interpret globes, and maps and plans at a variety of scales: the work should include using co-ordinates and four-figure grid references, measuring direction and distance, following routes etc..."	"use and interpret maps and plans at a variety of scales, including Ordnance Survey 1:25,000 and 1:50,000 maps: the work should include using six-figure grid references, following routes, identifying relief and landscape features, drawing cross-sections, and using maps in decision-making exercises."
		"make effective use of globes and atlases to find appropriate information and to locate places..."
		"select and use appropriate graphical techniques to present evidence on maps and diagrams, *eg pie charts, choropleth maps*"
"use secondary sources, *eg pictures, photographs (including aerial photographs) ....* to obtain geographical information"	"use secondary sources of evidence - pictures, photographs (including aerial photographs)..."	"select and use secondary sources of evidence, - photographs (including vertical and oblique aerial photographs), satellite images..."

Figure 5.6 Progression in graphicacy in the National Curriculum programmes of study (DfE. 1995)

Figure 5.6 tabulates some aspects of progression in graphicacy between key stages, as described in the National Curriculum programmes of study, though as you can see it still leaves many decisions to be made by the teacher. One of these decisions is the context in which the chosen aspect of graphicacy is to be developed. Remember that, as we saw in Chapter 3, it is important to develop skills in the context of the study of places and themes. It is also important to remember that individual learners will develop graphicacy at different speeds and to different levels. It will therefore be important to make provision for differentiation in this, as in other aspects of your teaching of geography.

Clearly opportunities to develop graphicacy are closely connected to the availability of appropriate resources, though many maps, photographs and diagrams can be gathered from newspapers and other 'consumable' sources. Bailey and Fox (1996, p.109) suggest that "*a useful exercise is to help pupils to collect different types of map and to incorporate them into displays dealing with the theme of 'different uses of maps'.*"

It is also important to remember that maps drawn by others are but one source for the development of graphicacy. Equally important are maps and diagrams drawn by the individual learner, for instance the sketch map of the school grounds as a basis for investigations into the quality of the school environment, or the route an individual takes to school. Sketch maps can also be a means of investigating individuals' **'mental maps'**, themselves indicative of the 'private geographies' held by individuals and which were mentioned in Chapter 3.

Resources for the development of graphicacy vary enormously in their sophistication. Somewhere near one end of the spectrum is the play-mat with the streets and shops of an imaginary town marked on it and model vehicles to play with, or the model farm with movable trees, buildings, animals and fences. Somewhere near the other end of the spectrum is the geographic information system (GIS) which is a powerful computer program enabling the collection, storage, retrieval, transformation and display of spatial information. The GIS program links maps with spatial information from databases or spreadsheets, enabling for instance the analysis of distribution of petrol filling stations in relation to volume of traffic flow over a road network. The computer draws particular maps of the data as required and displays them on the monitor screen. These maps can be manipulated, printed out or transferred into another application, eg a desktop publishing package for compiling a report of a geographical investigation.

Boardman (1983, p.19) makes the point that maps and aerial photographs are communication systems. They take information from reality and 'encode' it by way of symbols. The task for the user (the receiver) is to 'decode' the information. This decoding can be hampered by the amount of other information which is not immediately relevant to the task in hand. The relevant information is the 'signal', and that which is not relevant can be thought of as 'noise'. The relationship between the two is the 'signal-to-noise ratio'. An inexperienced user of, say, vertical aerial photographs, will have difficulty picking out semi-detached houses ('signal') because of all the other distracting information ('noise') which is provided. Part of the development of graphicacy lies in helping learners to develop filtering and focusing skills in order to improve the signal-to-noise ratio.

Graphicacy is also concerned with spatial relationships between, say, variables on a two- (or sometimes three-) dimensional graph. (Balchin and Coleman,1973, p.80) This spatial display of data in a graph frame may be used to show time scales and rates of change, eg a line graph of population growth and decline. Many of the diagrams in this book use spatially-organised information to make or emphasise a point which could not easily be made using words alone. For instance, those diagrams in which I have used overlapping circles are very similar to the technique of using Venn diagrams, itself a particularly spatial means of demonstrating relationships between 'sets' of information or data. This aspect of graphicacy brings geography into contact, indeed overlap, with mathematics, but the greater share of responsibility for developing all-round graphicacy rests with geography.

Graphicacy, then, is a central element of geography, and geography makes a unique contribution to the development of this important skill area. Spatial information is of enormous significance in geography, and will put in an appearance in the majority of lessons dealing with some aspect of the subject. The development of graphicacy should therefore permeate the geography curriculum, both as an explicitly articulated set of aims, objectives and learning activities in its own right, and also in the form of the resource material used to support other aspects of geographical study and investigation.

Activity

1. Study **Figure 5.6** carefully. How many aspects of progression in graphicacy can you identify in these extracts from the programmes of study for geography?

2. Discuss progression in graphicacy with someone responsible for geography in the school (probably the head of department in a secondary school or subject co-ordinator in a primary school). Some questions to guide you might be:
   - To what extent is the development of graphicacy systematically fostered through the teaching of geography in the school?
   - What resources are available to support this aspect of teaching and learning in geography ?
   - Is there co-ordination of the work of different teachers of geography in this aspect of their teaching?
   - How well-integrated is the work into studies of places and themes?
   - Is there co-ordination between geography and other subject areas, eg mathematics in matters relating to scale, co-ordinate systems etc?

3. Consider a sequence of lessons which you have either taught recently or are about to teach.
   - What assumptions have you made about your students' levels of graphicacy?
   - What part does the development of graphicacy play in the sequence of lessons?
   - What opportunities are there for your students to improve or consolidate their skills in graphicacy?
   - To what extent does your work allow for differentiation on the basis of graphicacy?

4. Consider your professional skills and competences as a teacher of geography.
   - What particular professional skills do you need to use in order to support the development of graphicacy among those whom you teach?
   - Does this suggest any areas for improvement as regards your own professional development?
   - Set yourself targets to guide your professional development as a teacher of graphicacy.

6

Assessment, recording and reporting

"Friday, April 3rd. Got full marks in the geography test today, Yes, I am proud to report that I got twenty out of twenty! I was also complimented on the neat presentation of my work. There is nothing I don't know about the Norwegian leather industry."

From' The Secret Diary of Adrian Mole aged 13³/₄', Sue Townsend, 1984

Aims

The purpose of this Chapter is to consider aspects of assessment, recording and reporting as they relate to your work as a teacher of geography, and in particular to your professional development. Never far from the focus of interest, these aspects of the teacher's work have been particularly in the spotlight with the introduction of National Curriculum arrangements. These arrangements have been based on twin statutory foundations of programmes of study (material to be covered) and attainment targets (descriptions of expected standards of attainment) and associated statutory assessment arrangements. In addition, there are now specified competences for new teachers. The assessment and recording of progress is an area of competence common to all schedules in use in the countries of the United Kingdom.

The nature of assessment

The quotation which opens this chapter draws attention to the aspect which tends to spring to mind when assessment is mentioned: the 'test'. But, though the test still has a place in the broader nature of assessment, understandings of assessment and what it means have changed. The word 'assessment' now carries a wider range of possibilities, implications and associations than perhaps ever before:

- *assessment is now seen as **a process**, rather than just as an event;*
- *formal assessment processes now tend to include **continuous assessment** rather than relying on a single terminal assessment;*
- ***formative assessment processes** are now widely used and valued, in addition to summative processes;*
- *assessment is now seen as something which can **involve learners in self- and peer-assessment** and the evaluation of their own progress, rather than assessment being something which is invariably done to them;*
- *assessment is no longer associated primarily with testing, but **fulfils a range of purposes** (Brown, 1994, pages 270-1);*
- *current assessment practices tend to emphasise **criterion-referencing**, as distinct from the norm-referencing of the past;*
- *assessment is a more open process and **criteria are more widely shared**, including with learners;*
- *assessment gives greater emphasis to **positive achievement**, ie what an individual knows, understands and can do;*
- *assessment is now seen as encompassing **a wider range of attributes** than was previously the case;*
- *assessment takes place in both formal and **less formal settings**;*
- *it is now part of the **professional responsibility of all teachers** to be involved in the formal assessment role (as distinct from day-to-day, on-going assessment), through the making of end-of-key-stage teacher assessments, and the marking of GCSE coursework and 'A' level individual studies;*
- *assessment now takes account of **a greater range of evidence** than was previously the case, including ephemeral evidence (ie 'short-lived' evidence, for instance oral contributions to a group discussion)*
- *it is now recognised that assessment practices vary in the extent to which they offer **equality of opportunity,** (see eg Lambert, 1996, pages 194-5) due to a greater understanding of the roles of gender, culture and language, etc.*

The list of attributes of assessment given here contains a number of terms which you may need to explore further. Kyriacou (1991, pages 109 - 111) contains a useful glossary of several important terms associated with assessment.

Action Point
Ensure that you have a firm grasp of the language of assessment. This is essential if you are to participate in discussions about assessment with colleagues, and to come to influence policy in schools where you work.

You will also need to be able to discuss assessment matters with parents who now have a more extensive knowledge of assessment.

Professional learning

*The processes and changes described in the quotation (right) apply not only to young people's learning, but also to professional development in general and to your professional learning in teaching in particular. Thus you may well move from an initial base-line competence as an NQT through **subject leader** and perhaps ultimately to '**advanced skills teacher**' status which reflect the development in your competences and personal achievements over several years in your career.*

*In some cases you may wish to seek other accreditation, for instance through **accreditation of prior experiential learning (APEL)** schemes which contribute to the award of a higher degree. You will find more about this in **Workbook 6** of the Beginning Teaching Workbooks series.*

These changes cannot be viewed in isolation. Rather, they are part of a broader current of change in education which has implications for the meanings we attach not only to the term 'assessment' but also to the roles of 'teacher' and 'learner':

> "*Education and training continue to move away from the use of the human mind as a store for information towards using the mind for sorting, synthesizing, discriminating and applying information which is already stored elsewhere. There is also continued movement away from assessing which is based on examinations taken on a particular day to classify, order and rank people, towards assessing which looks for competency and personal achievements over a period of time. The onus for learning is being shifted from the teacher to the learner. The roles of teacher and learner are rapidly changing, with the teacher seen as a manager and organizer of learning rather than a presenter of knowledge.*"

> *Harris and Bell, 1994, p.8*

Against this background of change in the "who, what, where, why, when and how" of assessment, it is clearly an important aspect of your professional development as a teacher of geography that you not only know and understand the aspects of assessment identified in this section in the general sense, but that you also recognise their significance within whatever geography teaching is part of your responsibilities.

Activity

1. Research the assessment policy and practices employed to support the teaching and learning of geography in your school.
2. How many of the attributes listed in the bulleted list on the previous page can you detect in the way in which assessment in geography is conducted in your school? Is this typical of other approaches to assessment in the school?

The purposes of assessment

> "*Much assessment is a waste of time because it has no clear purpose. Any assessment should be an attempt to find the answer to a question. Usually, that question is: "What should I do next?"*

> *Dockerell 1995, p.292*

Lambert (p.188) notes that 'fitness for purpose' is a key idea when considering assessment. In your thinking about assessment it will therefore be important to be clear about the purpose before coming to a decision about the appropriateness of the approach under consideration. There are four widely recognised purposes of assessment: (see, eg Marsden, 1994, p.78)

*   **formative**, *in which the aim is to provide information to teachers, learners and others for the purpose of supporting future learning (**diagnostic assessment** is an aspect of formative processes, in that it seeks to provide information to guide support and remediation);*
*   **summative**, *in which the aim is to provide a summary of the individual's attainment at a point in time, eg at the end of a course;*
*   **certification**, *in which the aim is to provide the means of qualifying or providing some public recognition and to enable selection (it is normally based on summative assessment);*
*   **quality control**, *where information derived from assessment is used in evaluation procedures.*

In practice, as indicated by some of the clarifications given above, these categories are by no means mutually exclusive. For instance, the end-of-key-stage assessments associated with the National Curriculum are summative for the key stage concluded, but are also intended to feed information about individuals forward formatively into the next key stage. Further, in their aggregated form (including the controversial league tables), the assessments provide evaluation data about the performance of schools and local authorities, though the value of such information as a fair and reliable basis for comparisons is contested.

The quotation from Dockerell which opens this section makes the point that for much of the time assessment should be an integral part of teaching and learning. This does **not** mean incessant testing, however. What it does mean is that the teacher should constantly be evaluating the outcomes of the teaching and learning which has taken place, through whatever means are appropriate. Assessment fulfils an important role in the cycle of 'plan-do-review' when viewed this way: without it the next turn of the cycle is disconnected from the previous turn. Like Janus, the Roman god of doors, such assessment looks in two directions: back into the work which has been done, and forward into what to do next. This is because such assessment is guided by the learning objectives which the teacher has identified and is set within a context of continuity and progression. By focusing on individual progress it guides differentiation.

"Most schools recognise the importance of relating assessment to curriculum planning. The main weakness in much of the medium and short-term planning is the lack of clear learning objectives which can be assessed." (OFSTED, 1996ᵃ, p.38)

A simple example will serve to demonstrate. One of the learning objectives in geography being worked towards in a KS2 class is that children will be able to use an alphanumeric coordinate system to locate squares on a plan of the school grounds. The children are working in pairs to identify each square and find out what is in it. Through observation the teacher notes that, while the majority of the class can find the correct map-squares through careful effort, some children are having no difficulty and are not being challenged by the activity. The teacher sets these children an extension task in which they use a town plan of a less familiar place and which contains more information (a lower ratio of 'signal to noise'). Others in the class continue with the activity using the plan of the school grounds.

This admittedly simple example makes the point that this sort of assessment is an on-going, natural part of how the teacher works. Indeed, it is hard to see how one could teach at all without engaging in this sort of naturalistic assessment, as its purpose is to support individual children's learning on a day-to-day basis. The process may be supported by notes made by the teacher, but a great deal of the assessment data gathered through such naturalistic processes is held in the teacher's head and up-dated with every activity in which the child engages, confirming or modifying the picture of the child's capabilities, needs and attainment which is developing. Teachers who truly 'know their children' know a great deal more than their names!

The kind of assessment described in the previous three paragraphs is formative assessment, mostly of a diagnostic type. Another aspect of formative assessment is more subtle, dealing with individual motivation and the development of self-awareness and of the intellectual autonomy mentioned in the previous Chapter. This is done through giving individuals a role in assessing their own work. This is not just a matter of having a list of right answers to factual questions and making them available for individuals to mark their own or one-another's work (though there is of course a place for this). Rather, what is being indicated here is that "good teaching is typified by good planning with clear objectives **shared with pupils**." (OFSTED, 1996ᵇ, p.12, my emphasis.)

Children need to know what they are seeking to achieve so that they know when they have achieved it! This is in line with the earlier quotation form Harris and Bell about "the onus for learning being shifted... to the learner". Of course the objectives have to be expressed as learning outcomes or assessment criteria for a piece of work, and in language which the learners can understand and can relate to the task.

This should not be taken to mean that the teacher will not want to see the work! But it does enable learners to begin to take a higher degree of responsibility for their own learning and to become partners in the process rather than passive recipients of judgements made by the teacher in relation to obscure, unstated or, worse, unthought-of criteria. Clearly stated criteria provide the basis for feedback to the learner about her/his performance on the task, and Stern (1995, p.79) notes that having clear criteria links closely with the idea of assessment being *fair*, itself an important consideration.

Activity

1. Think about your own teaching, and in particular some learning activities or tasks you have set recently. Did you make the objectives and/or criteria clear to your students? If not, consider how you can build this in to some activities and tasks you are currently planning.
2. Evaluate whether making objectives/criteria clearer seems to make a difference to the standard of work achieved.

Marking

Marking follows on naturally from the previous section. In summative assessment marking means the award of marks to provide a total, intended in some way to summarise and sum up the individual's performance, as in examination marking, for instance. Of course, most of a teacher's marking is not of this type. Most marking is formative in intent. It is therefore to be seen as part of a broader current of **feedback** from the teacher to individuals and groups about their work and progress.

Whatever system of symbols (ticks, crosses, question marks, exclamation marks, asterisks, squiggles, underlinings, arrows, vertical bars in the margin, abbreviations etc.) you use, remember that you are engaging in a form of communication, primarily with the learner but quite possibly also with others with an interest in their work (parents, other teachers). Your attempt to communicate has failed if your message remains obscure (and this goes for the legibility of your handwriting too!). Remember too that what you are marking belongs to someone else. Show that you value what they have produced by how you treat it, even if it is also necessary to be critical of the work.

If the objectives and criteria for a piece of work are clear then the teacher's comment on that work, whether oral or written, can address those objectives and criteria as indicated in **Figure 6.1**. This enables confirmation to be given where the criteria are met or the objectives achieved, and guidance to be given where they are not. Clear objectives enable a dialogue to take place between teacher and student, focused on the work which has been done.

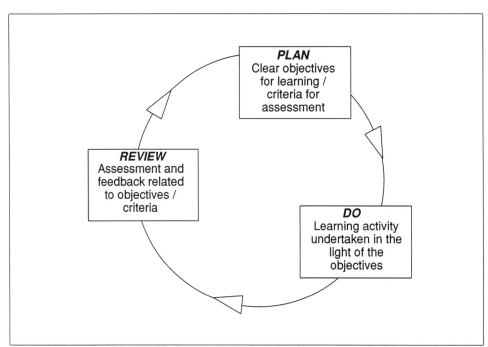

Figure 6.1 The role of objectives in planning, doing and marking work

This sounds easier than it is. To write full, formative feedback on large numbers of individual pieces of work is immensely time-consuming. This can be problematic as it is generally recognised that in order to have much meaning and formative impact, the feedback needs to be given quickly. "Assessment should have an effect on future work. The effect is inversely proportional to the time gap between work and assessment." (Stern, 1996, p.80) It is not an overstatement to say that for some teachers the management of their marking is one of the most intractable of the professional challenges they face (and you may well recognise the voice of experience here!)

Alternatively feedback about work can be oral or, better still, a dialogue. This again sounds easier than it is. Lambert (1996, p.192) recognises the value of "subject-based conversations with individual pupils", but also notes (with perhaps a hint of understatement) that "there are challenging classroom management issues for teachers to overcome" in providing such opportunities. Nevertheless, bearing in mind the changes in the roles of teacher and learner pointed to in the quotation from Harris and Bell earlier in this Chapter, it may well be that the opportunity for such conversations will be found through the use of approaches employing aspects of **flexible learning** and **supported self-study**.

These approaches enable the teacher to take on more the role of a **tutor**. Some of the ground for this has been prepared by the now familiar review and target-setting activities associated with Records of Achievement (ROA) procedures. One can begin to see how openness on the part of the teacher about clearly articulated objectives and criteria would enable more peer and self-assessment by students. This would enable them to take increased responsibility for their own learning, and to develop increasing autonomy. Dialogues with the teacher/tutor would now be important in supporting the process. The emphasis here would most definitely be on learning and how best to support it, rather than on traditional conceptions of teaching as 'telling'.

An interesting conclusion to be drawn from the above discussion is that questions of assessment and marking are ultimately inseparable from issues around the choice of approach to teaching and learning. A clear, informed, personal philosophy about these matters is important to you, as to each and every teacher, if you are to participate in discussions and decisions leading to the creation of school (or department) policies, and in the practical expression of such policies through your day-to-day work as a teacher.

Activity

1. Review your own approach to marking. How closely does it conform to any school or departmental policy on marking?
2. Investigate the amount of time you spend marking in a typical week. How much of this marking would you say has what Lambert (p.194) calls **consequential validity,** ie, has real consequences in terms of individuals' learning and progress? If you find this question difficult to answer, you may wish to design and carry out a small piece of research into this aspect of your work: discuss it with your mentor, professional tutor or HE tutor. If you are involved in your school's appraisal system, it might make an interesting appraisal focus.
3. Review your use of time and approach to classroom management. Can you make more opportunities to discuss work with individuals and groups? This might be a useful focus for discussions, particularly as part of a development being explored by an interested group of teachers.

Recording

Recording goes hand-in-hand with marking. And it is important to remember, as with marking, that how recording should be done is for schools and teachers to decide. There are no centrally designed and imposed systems. Further, remember that it is not necessary or productive to try to record everything. Here again, the test of fitness for purpose comes into play, this time in two ways:

- *why am I recording this particular information (what is it for?);*
- *am I recording it in the most appropriate manner?*

At one time the teacher's mark book would be the most familiar recording device. It is still important, but has now been supplemented by computer-based systems, eg spreadsheets, and increasingly also by ROA-type processes where a file or portfolio of items is built up. The main evaluative questions to ask about any recording system are:

- *does it allow you to record useful information easily?*
- *does it enable easy access to and retrieval of the information recorded?*

You will probably wish to record the following types of information:

- *presence at/absence from lessons (indeed this is a matter of policy in most schools);*
- *grade, mark or other summary information about classwork;*
- *whether any homework was set, whether it was handed in, summary information about the standard of the work;*

Flexible learning and tutoring
For more about these approaches see:
- *Philip Waterhouse (1991) Flexible Learning*
- *Robert Powell (1991) Resources for Flexible Learning*
- *Philip Waterhouse (1991) Tutoring*
- *Mike Hughes (1993) Flexible Learning: Evidence Examined*
  all published by Network Education Press.
- *Supported Self Study (Bob Rainbow, 1989) is a book for workshop and in-service training providers which contains some useful background and ideas about supported self-study approaches.*

Students' work

Do not forget that a very important record of an individual's work is the work itself, whether built up in an exercise book, a file, a folder, a tray (or even on a floppy disc!) Increasingly attention is focused on the compiling and maintaining of portfolios of work. It is stressed that these should be manageable (ideally by the students themselves, perhaps as an aspect of termly review and target-setting) and contain only illustrative samples of work, chosen to represent the current 'personal best'.

Alternatively, a portfolio might contain pointers to where the work can be located (eg by use of a proforma filled in by the student to indicate the date title and teacher comment for a chosen piece in an exercise book, which then need be neither cut out nor photocopied) (Grimwade, 1996, p.207).

"You may wish to keep some examples so that you can discuss a pupil's work with parents and other teachers, but there is no statutory requirement to keep detailed records or evidence on every pupil." (Sir Ron Dearing, SCAA 1996, p.i)

- any 'commendations' given or positive or negative referrals made, together with other intermittent information about individuals (note that there may be a separate system for this information).

This information will be recorded on a lesson-by-lesson basis. In addition you will also want to record periodically:

- scores for any formal assessment set;
- summary grades given as part of any school reporting system.

Some teachers mix these last two categories of information in with other mark-book information whereas others record it on separate sheets, sometimes in a more centralised system as a reflection of school or departmental policy.

Overall whatever individual recording system is used it is worth remembering that it should work alongside any school and/or departmental systems in such a way that the two complement one another without unnecessary duplication or waste of effort. Remember too that a great deal of information is not formally recorded anywhere, in the sense of being written down: it is carried in teachers' heads. This is particularly the case with **ephemeral evidence** of what students know, understand and can do, as indicated by their questions and answers, their contributions to discussion and any other observed information (including their actions, practical and collaborative skills and other behavioural attributes).

Activity

1. Apply the two pairs of questions (see the first two pairs of bullet points, above) to the information you record, and to the system which you use. How well does your system perform?
2. Compare your approach to recording with that of a colleague. If you are working in a situation where everyone uses an agreed system as a matter of departmental or school policy, it might be interesting to 'compare notes' with someone from another department or school. (If you are reading this as a student teacher, you should have potential access to a large number of systems as experienced by your student colleagues. Marking and recording processes might prove to be an excellent theme for pooling your various experiences in a workshop session when you meet together as a group.

Reporting

The purpose of reporting is to make a summary statement of an individual's progress to date, in this case in geography. This summary will normally include reference to what has been achieved as well as diagnostic comments pointing to areas for improvement. The precise format of a report and conventions regarding the use of grades, marks and other summary information are matters normally determined by school policy, itself reflecting and incorporating statutory requirements. You will be working within the context set by such a policy.

When writing reports it is most important to bear in mind the **audience** for whom the report is being written. This in turn will influence:

- the information you include;
- the vocabulary you use;
- the language register you adopt.

Normally parents/guardians spring to mind as the audience for reports, though of course they are not the sole audience: even if they receive the report in a sealed envelope they do not usually keep it to themselves! In practice most reporting is more open than this, with learners involved to a greater or lesser degree in the process, as shown on **Figure 6.2**. Indeed, many teachers see the report as representing a dialogue between themself and the individual about whom the report is written.

Increasing learner input into the reporting process →

| Confidential report to parent/s or guardian/s | Child sees report before parent/s or guardian/s | Report used as basis for teacher/student discussion | Student invited to write a comment; teacher comment responds | Negotiated statement from student and teacher |

Figure 6.2 A spectrum of learner involvement in the reporting process

Grimwade (1996, p.207) notes that one of the particular challenges of report writing is that very often one is writing for several audiences at the same time. We have already established that this includes **parents** and **children**. This multiple audience can also include **other teachers** (in many cases a copy of the report is filed for reference; in the secondary school the subject teachers' reports are usually read by the form tutor and head of year in preparation for them writing their comments, and for monitoring purposes.) If a child moves to **another school**, either in the case of primary to secondary transfer, (or first to middle to high school or other local variants), or because he/she moves house, reports are an important means of supporting continuity and progression of educational experience. Also, particularly in the case of older students, **prospective employers** form part of the audience for subject reports.

The information you include will in part reflect the school's policy. It may include an agreed system of alphanumeric grades, (in which case stick to the way in which the school's system operates). It may also include information derived from test or examination marks, classwork and homework (and formally assessed coursework in the case of GCSE and A Level courses). You should also include aspects which are particular to geography, for instance the development of certain skills (eg, investigation/enquiry, fieldwork, map-reading), and the development of knowledge and understanding of places and themes. At the end of a key stage the National Curriculum 'level' of attainment must also be reported.

You will probably also want to include comment on some of the cross-curricular skills, such as the use of IT, discussion, team-working, written expression and accuracy, study/information skills. Also, there will be a place for comments relating to attitude (enthusiasm, initiative, willingness to cooperate, etc as appropriate) which gives you the opportunity to personalise the report further.

The information should be balanced. Stern (1995 p.86) notes that many reports "follow the 'positive comments only, plus targets' pattern of criterion-referenced assessment". Certainly a wholly negative report makes depressing reading and offers little by way of incentive for improvement, nor indication of how to improve. Equally, a wholly enthusiastic report, though unlikely to be depressing to read, may fall into the same trap of not supporting improvement. As the comments from inspection findings indicate (see margin), it is important to give a full, honest picture of strengths and weaknesses, achievements and areas for improvement (though there is a degree of divergence between this view of reports and the 'positives plus targets' ROA approach).

Inspection findings indicate that "schools generally provide useful reports for parents and statutory requirements are usually met. The improvements in reporting observed in recent years has continued, but there remains scope for refinement. In particular, many subject reports are unduly positive and fail to make constructive criticism. Such reports give the impression that attainment is better than it actually is." (OFSTED, 1996ᵃ,p.39, 1996ᵇ, p.40)

The vocabulary you use is important, as you will wish what you say to be accessible to its intended audience. Terminology which is in everyday use among teachers may be very obscure to parents and may come over as jargon. It is possible for school departments and even whole staffs to develop certain understandings and usages of particular words which may make outward communication difficult. The same is true of specific geographical terminology. There is a balance to be struck between the use of specialised language which is specific and appropriate to the matter being described, and the loss of important meanings through the use of less specialised language.

The register in which you write is very important. A report is a relatively formal document so, notwithstanding the general trend towards greater informality, it should have a relatively formal 'tone'. Colloquialisms, slang and informal writing are unlikely to be appropriate. On the other hand, space and time for writing are limited. Remember too that part of your audience is also the children about whom the report is written. Avoid complex constructions. Be succinct.

Information technology and report writing
Some teachers are now using comment banks, accessed via computers to produce reports. This usually reflects a whole-school decision to create reports in this way. This system has ensured the writing of quite full reports by some teachers, though others find it restrictive and impersonal to select from a bank of pre-determined comments.

Colleagues can check a sample of reports for you (or even a whole set if circumstances permit), in order to evaluate your report comments and legibility. It is also very important to maintain a high standard of technical accuracy (eg spellings, punctuation) so proof-read your reports carefully or, better still, arrange to swap with a colleague to proof-read one-another's. This is not just a matter of 'quality assurance' - you will learn from what they say and how they say it.

Increasingly reports are being drafted on word-processors, enabling automatic spell-checking and easy amendment if necessary. Comments can then easily be stored on disc until the next report is due, and new comments can be written in the light of the previous ones (this again is beneficial to supporting continuity and progression). When printed out, presentation and legibility of such reports is good, though they may appear somewhat less personal than a handwritten report.

Activity

1. If you are a student teacher, investigate your school's policy on reports.
   Draft a sample of reports for a few students whom you know well.
   Use the reports as a basis for discussion with your mentor or with their regular teacher.
2. Discuss school reports with a group of students.
   What are their 'likes' and 'dislikes' about school reports? What do they find useful?
   Note your findings and your own reactions and thoughts in your reflective journal.
3. Arrange a meeting with your professional tutor at which you will discuss a set of reports you have recently written. (Reporting is another possibility for an appraisal focus)

Assessment and progression

As already noted, assessment as an on-going process plays an important part in the cycle of plan-do-review. It is therefore closely involved with planning and monitoring for progression, and with indicating when specific differentiation is necessary with regard to individual learning.

Progression in school geography reflects and runs parrallel to the maturational changes which involve individuals' physical, intellectual, social and emotional development. The geography curriculum, as with all other aspects of the curriculum, must therefore reflect this through its planning.

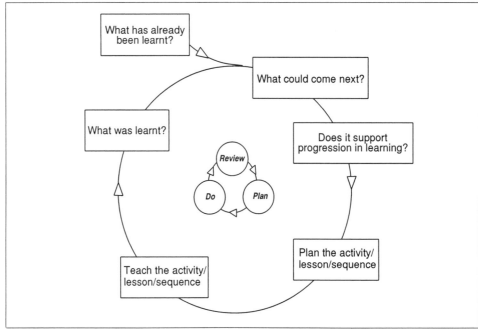

Figure 6.3 Assessment, planning and progression in geography

Figure 6.3 expresses the relationship between assessment, planning and progression in simplified diagrammatic form. In reality the relationship is somewhat 'messier' and more dynamic than what is shown here, but the diagram serves to emphasise the underlying structure, elements and direction of the process.

Bennetts (1986, p.160) notes how progression is a subtle idea, and one which focuses attention on "what pupils learn and the quality of that learning." Clearly in order to plan for progression in the manner summarised in **Figure 6.3**, you will need:

* to be able to identify the learning which individuals have achieved;
* to have a clear perception of the strands of learning to be developed within geography;
* to have a view on what it is reasonable to expect students of a given age to know, understand and be able to do.

In addition, it is important to have a clear perception of the strands of learning also to be developed within those **cross curricular elements** which are manifest in geographical work (see Chapter 7 for more about these).

There have been various attempts to pick out elements of progression in geography. Most show similarities with what HMI proposed in 1986 (DES, pages 39 - 40):

* increasing breadth of studies, extending content to different places, new landscapes etc;
* increasing depth of studies to include greater complexity and abstraction, moving from the concrete and observable to the theoretical and inferred;
* increasing spatial scale of areas studied;
* development of skills, including enquiry and specific techniques;
* increasing opportunity to examine social, economic, political and environmental issues, involving use of evidence and awareness of role of values, attitudes and beliefs.

These came to underlie much of the subsequent work on the National Curriculum for England and Wales in both its initial and revised form. SCAA's 'Dearing' Review gave more detail, as shown in **Figure. 6.4.**

Key Stage 1	Key Stage 2	Key Stage 3
Through the key stage pupils will increasingly: ● broaden and deepen their knowledge and understanding of places and themes; ● recognise and describe what places are like with appropriate geographical vocabulary; ● offer their own explanations for what they observe; ● make comparisons between places and between geographical features; ● develop and use appropriate geographical skills. *Source: SCAA 1994*	Through the key stage pupils will increasingly: ● broaden and deepen their knowledge and understanding of places and themes; ● recognise and describe what places are like with accuracy and coherence; ● offer explanations for the characteristics of places; ● identify physical and human processes and describe some of their effects; ● apply geographical ideas learnt in one context to other studies at the same scale; ● acquire information, from secondary sources as well as first-hand observation, to investigate aspects of local and more distant physical and human environments; ● develop and use appropriate geographical skills.	Through the key stage pupils will increasingly: ● broaden and deepen their knowledge and understanding of places and themes; ● make use of a wide and precise geographical vocabulary; ● analyse, rather than describe, geographical patterns, processes and change; ● appreciate the interactions within and between physical and human processes that operate in any environment; ● appreciate the interdependence of places; ● become proficient at conducting and comparing studies at a widening range of scales and in contrasting places and environments; ● apply their geographical knowledge and understanding to unfamiliar contexts; ● select and make effective use of skills and techniques to support their geographical investigations; ● appreciate the limitations of geographical geographical evidence and the tentative and incomplete nature of some explanations.

Figure 6.4 Progression across key stages in National Curriculum geography

Bennetts (1996, p. 85) suggests that it may be easier for schools to use the following headings as a basis for analysing scope for progression (see also Chapter 4, above):

- *breadth of geographical knowledge;*
- *depth of geographical understanding;*
- *use of geographical skills;*
- *attitudes and values.*

The level descriptions for geography in the National Curriculum (DFE, 1995, pages 18 - 20) embody aspects of progression in the subject and provide the basis for teachers to make judgements of individual attainment at the end of a key stage: they provide a 'pen portrait' of different levels of performance. There are eight levels, plus 'exceptional performance'. All aspects of a teacher's assessment of the performance of an individual feed into this judgement. Of course, it is also up to the teacher, through planning of work, monitoring and differentiation, to provide opportunities for individuals to demonstrate what they know, understand and can do in ways which enable fair and accurate judgements to be made.

A manageable view of key features of progression focuses on four broadly-defined aspects of geography (SCAA 1996, p. 4), each of which can be sub-divided into two strands of progression as shown in **Figure 6.5.**

For further detail about the features of progression illustrated in Figure 6.5 you are referred to the SCAA's **Exemplification of Standards** *(1996, pages 6 to 13). Though the examples given in the exemplification relate specifically to the KS3 programme of study, the level descriptions and nature of progression are analysed across the entire range of levels, providing clear and useful guidance.*

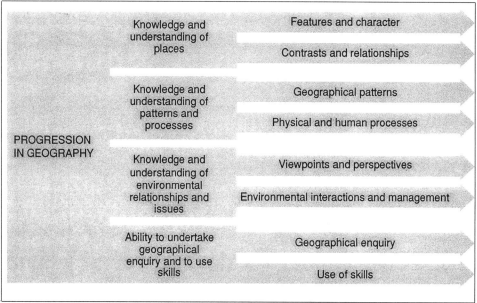

Figure 6.5 Aspects of progression in National Curriculum geography

Activity

1. Look back over the views of progression given in this section. Critically evaluate them. Which view of progression seems most appropriate and useful to you?
2. Ask a colleague (eg your peer partner) to read this section. Arrange to discuss the relationship between assessment, progression and planning with them.
3. Does your school or department have a key stage plan for geography? Analyse any such plan in the light of what you now understand about progression in the subject.
4. Focus on a sequence of lessons you have planned. To what extent does your sequence contribute to the development of any of the aspects of progression identified in **Figure 6.5**

7

Whole learner, whole curriculum

"It is not easy to sustain a sense of the whole.........

All too commonly the teacher teaches a particular subject or unit within a subject without any reference to its relationship to other components of the curriculum. Similarly the student may study one subject after another with no idea of what his growing fund of knowledge and skill might contribute to an integrated way of life. Students and teachers alike are prone to take the curriculum as they find it....... without ever inquiring into the comprehensive pattern within which the constituent parts are located."

Phenix, in Golby et al, 1975, p.165

Aims

The quotation which opens the Chapter suggests that it is both likely and undesirable for teachers and students to have a disconnected view of the curriculum. This Chapter therefore has three inter-linked purposes:

- *to examine the relationship between geography and other aspects of the 'whole curriculum';*
- *to consider some of the implications of this relationship for teaching and learning;*
- *to consider some of the implications for your professional development.*

In order to achieve these aims it is necessary to consider some of the underlying frameworks of attitudes, values and beliefs which influence the opinions and actions of those who seek to affect the way in which education is viewed and transacted. These underlying frameworks, whose effect is to formalise 'systems of ideas embodying strongly held beliefs and/or traditions' (Marsden, 1995, p.8) are **ideologies**, and as Marsden points out, "the more intensely held the ideology, the more rigid the stance taken. The current context of educational practice is manifestly one of warring ideologies."

The contested curriculum: ideologies in action

As became clear in the arguments which took place around the development of the National Curriculum, there is no clear consensus about the curriculum. Indeed, it is probably fair to say that the school curriculum, at least in England and Wales, was revealed as an ideological battleground in unprecedented ways. (see Chapter 2) All aspects of the curriculum (and geography was no exception) saw their share of controversy, as indeed did the curriculum as a whole. What should the curriculum look like? What, indeed, is it for?

Answers to questions like these reveal deep-seated 'ideological' positions with regard to education. Is education every child's birthright? Or is it society's means of ensuring a supply of people with the basic skills needed for employment? Is its purpose to change society, or to keep it as it is? Should education ask questions, or pass on knowledge and values? John Fien, cited by Hicks and Holden (1996, pages 7 - 8) suggests that there are three underlying ideologies of education:

- *conservative;*
- *reformative;*
- *transformative.*

An alternative four-way typology is proposed by Skilbeck, cited by Marsden (1995, p. 9):

- *classical humanism;*
- *utilitarianism;*
- *progressivism;*
- *reconstructionism.*

The two classifications are summarised in **Figure 7.1**. Both sets of descriptions are simplifications, of course, but both identify some important aspects of the very foundations of the way in which people think about education.

Conservative

- Schools prepare students for work

- Existing social, economic and political structures are legitimised and maintained

- Classrooms and subject teaching organised along formal lines

- Dominant approach is directive transmission of knowledge

- Purpose: to learn your place

After Hicks & Holden (1995)

Reformative

- School prepares individuals to participate in reform of society

- Classrooms are more informal and individualised

- Less rigid subject framework

- Learning is person-centred and facilitative

- Purpose: to learn who you are

Transformative

- School and society reflect one another; flexible boundaries between school and community

- School plays a part in challenging social, political and economic inequalities

- Mixed ability group work dominates

- Dominant role of teacher is as resource person

- Purpose: to transform self and society

Classical humanism

- Promotes and passes on traditional values
- Subject-centred conception of curriculum
- Traditionally restricted to elitist and academicist goals
- Purpose: to hand on cultural heritage

Utilitarianism

- Social well-being is achieved through wealth accumulation and consumerism
- Focuses on instruction and training
- Goals are seen in terms of economic utility

- Purpose: train pupils to take their place unquestioningly in pursuit of national economic goals

Progressivism

- Overtly child-centred

- Discovery learning is emphasised
- Childhood is important in its own right, not as a preparation for adulthood
- Purpose: to develop personal autonomy

After Marsden (1995)

Reconstructionism

- Seeks to interpret, understand and anticipate social change
- Distinctions between subjects are blurred
- Moral education and social values are stressed

- Purpose: harmonious integration of individuals and society

Figure 7.1 Educational ideologies: two possible typologies

Of course, it is perfectly possible for an individual, a school or a government to display aspects of more than one ideology, so these categories should not be seen as mutually exclusive. Rather, they often reflect orientations or 'leanings' in a manner which is somewhat analogous to the way in which individuals have a preferred learning style. (Learning styles are discussed in detail in **Beginning Teaching Workbook 3**, Tolley et al, 1996).

Ideologies influence how geography is seen as a subject, both in its own right and in relation to the curriculum as a whole. In order to engage in curriculum debate and development it is important to be aware of this, and to be able to recognise the ideological positions underlying the arguments advanced by others (and, indeed, by oneself). For instance, teaching about industrial change or the role of multi-national companies could be very different in the hands of a teacher who had predominantly conservative leanings and one who had predominantly transformative views. Equally, a teacher with progressive or reconstructionist leanings is more likely to investigate links with other subject areas than one from the classical humanist viewpoint, who is more likely to stress the distinctiveness of geography as a subject and the need to preserve its unique identity.

At a different scale of operation, we could agree with Marsden that comprehensive schools were born of a reconstructionist view of schooling (equality of opportunity for all), whereas selective schools could be said to reflect the classical humanist view (the best for the most able - or the most able to pay, in the case of independent schools). Vocational education can in such an analysis be seen as a utilitarian prescription for 'the rest'.

Activity

1. Analyse a copy of your school's prospectus or brochure.
   Which ideology/ideologies does it appear to reflect?
   Is this consistent with what actually happens in the school?
   Are the school's values consistent with your own educational values?
2. What values would you say underlie the teaching of geography in your school?
   Do these reflect the dominance of any particular ideological position?
   Where do you stand on the teaching of geography?

Geography and the whole curriculum

Part of your development as a teacher is to gain a greater understanding of the nature, purpose and operation of a school's curriculum. In the Chapter 'Taking a closer look at the whole curriculum' in **Beginning Teaching Workbook 3** (Tolley et al, 1996), we quoted a definition from the Nottinghamshire County Council Statement of Curriculum Entitlement which included the sentence: "*For pupils in school at any stage the curriculum is the sum of all that they experience*", and we attempted to summarise the components of the whole curriculum diagramatically thus:

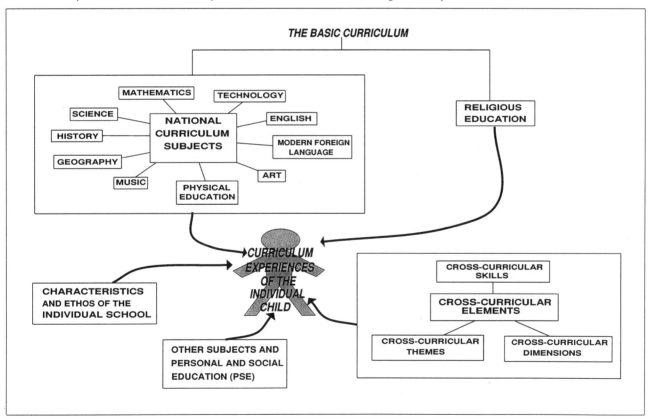

Figure 7.2 Some aspects of the whole curriculum (Tolley et al, 1996, Workbook 3, p. 37)

Of course the diagram cannot represent the complexity of all the interlinking and overlapping which take place in producing the total curriculum experience. Rather, the intention of **Figure 7.2** is to identify at least some of the parts which comprise the curriculum. These parts interact and together constitute the complex, dynamic 'whole curriculum'.

In the context of this Chapter we are interested in the interaction between geography and some of those other component parts. Some of those interactions are summarised in **Figure 7.3.**

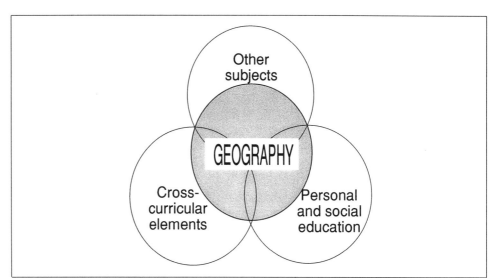

Figure 7.3 The relationship between geography and other aspects of the curriculum

This relationship is of course complex and dynamic, and the diagram again a simplification. This complexity is due in no small part to geography's own nature; indeed, "geography is a wide field of study, a feat of curriculum integration in itself". (Knight, 1993, p.48)

Geography and other subjects

Geography as a separate discipline has an interesting relationship with other subjects. Though geography, as we have seen, has its own internal history as 'a contested enterprise' (Livingstone, 1992), its relationship with other subjects and/or disciplines has never been particularly clear. Viewed positively, this has put geography in a chairing rôle 'at the meeting of all the subjects', or at least as a 'bridging subject' between the Arts and the Sciences. Less positively, geography has been viewed as a 'jackdaw subject', gathering up shiny bits of other subject areas, having little by way of a clear or distinctive identity of its own.

In Hirst's analysis the main 'forms of knowledge' are characterised by possessing both distinctive conceptual structures and distinctive principles of procedure. These would be of great significance in education, and would both underlie and be reflected in curriculum objectives. Because of the extent of available knowledge in each 'form', it is particularly important that these curriculum objectives, and the methodology chosen to reach them, reflect each form's distinctive procedures.

These views can be traced at least in part to Paul Hirst's analysis of human knowledge (Hirst, 1965) and its systemisation into 'forms of knowledge', of which the curriculum is a microcosm. Such forms (Hirst proposed eight) include mathematics, the physical sciences and religion. Geography, by Hirst's analysis, has insufficient coherence or distinctiveness to be a separate form of knowledge. Rather, geography would be a 'field of knowledge', cutting across and drawing from several forms, "held together simply by (its) subject matter". (Wynne, 1973, p.253)

What this means is that geography, almost by definition, will draw from other subjects as necessary to progress and enhance whatever enquiry is in progress. In true post-modern fashion, geography will constantly resonate with references to other subject areas, whether explicitly acknowledged or not, the permeability of its bounds the only sure thing. Thus the teacher of geography is in a particularly good position to link with, draw from and contribute to work in other subject areas.

Unsurprisingly, therefore, such links have indeed occurred, with differing degrees of formalisation, at both local and national scales. I have referred earlier (page 40) to the Schools Council project, *Place, Time and Society 8-13* (Blyth et al, 1976) in which geography was regarded, along with other social subjects, as a resource for building an appropriate curriculum. There have been other instances of this type of interdisciplinary approach to curriculum planning in all phases of education, including much primary 'topic' work. For students at key stage 4, 'humanities', including aspects of history and geography, is available as an examination option at GCSE. Marsden (1994, p.107) provides an example where geography is combined with art and history to produce a topic focus.

In the earlier section on graphicacy (pages 52-53) I have touched briefly on geography's association with mathematics. Kenyon (1994, p.121) takes this further, linking geography, science and mathematics in the primary curriculum by way of enquiry-based study. Geography, not least because of its use of quantified data in the form of area, distance, and absolute and ratio statistical information, can make a great contribution to the cross-curricular core skill of numeracy, itself important in both school-based learning and in life in general.

Geography can link usefully with work in modern foreign languages. Some use of the language brings authenticity to geographical studies of distant places (eg the PGCE geography student who welcomed his year nine geography class to the lesson as a Japanese teacher would, in Japanese, and taught them how to respond accordingly). Wiegand (1992, pages 194-6) describes a lesson in a primary topic on Germany in which he uses the German language to enhance the lesson. As this book goes to press the European BILD project (bilingual integration of languages and disciplines) is in its first year. Under this project trainee teachers in a variety of 'non-linguistic disciplines', including geography, have the opportunity to train to teach their discipline though the medium of a modern foreign language. Some secondary schools are also experimenting with this approach.

There are many other possible, beneficial links, some of which are indicated elsewhere in this book. My aim here has been to alert you to some of the possibilities in the hope that you will discover others for yourself. By its nature the notion of linking a changing discipline with other disciplines, themselves undergoing change and development, is dynamic.

Activity

1. Choose another subject area from the curriculum and actively investigate the actual and potential links with geography by talking to the other subject's coordinator / head of department / subject teacher.
2. In order to focus your discussions it may help if you have a preliminary meeting at which you exchange outline descriptions and core objectives of geography and the other chosen subject.
3. Plan together a piece of teaching and learning which explicitly addresses both subject areas. (Alternatively, if you have a peer partner this would be a good opportunity for some collaborative work with her/him.)
4. Teach the work in the normal way. If possible, build in some joint observation. Then have a joint review discussion at which you evaluate the work.
   - What effect has this approach had on the quality of learning?
   - What have you learnt about the relationship between the two subject areas?
   - Can you now see improvements to be made to the work you have done, or further possibilities for development?

Geography and personal and social education (PSE)

> "Personal and social education is the intentional promotion of the personal and social development of pupils through the whole curriculum and the whole school experience."

Watkins, quoted by Thacker 1995, p.260

Geography can play an important part in the personal and social development (PSD) of the individual. Of course, it is possible to teach geography in such a way as to minimise its contribution to these processes - or to maximise it.

Thacker (p.265) quotes five factors drawn from school effectiveness research which are particularly important for PSD. One of these factors is the encouragement of active participation of young people in lessons, and the existence of conditions allowing them to use their own initiative to carry out their own lines of enquiry. Elsewhere in this book I have drawn attention to active learning and the development of autonomy (pages 50-51) and to the enquiry approach (pages 21-24). We can see that if you are stressing the use of these approaches in your planning and teaching of geography, you will be providing valuable opportunities for PSD.

This is equally true in all phases of education. It is a matter of underlying philosophies of education (themselves reflecting ideologies) and their expression through curriculum processes of teaching and learning, rather than the more superficial business of timetables and the labels which are given to slots of time (though this of course also gives 'messages'.) The secondary school often has

"Innumeracy, an inability to deal comfortably with the fundamental notions of number and chance, plagues far too many otherwise knowledgeable citizens."
(John Allen Paulos, 1988)

a PSE programme identified and articulated. Such a programme may take place in a time-tabled lesson or in 'tutor time'. But if the rest of the curriculum does not also support and work towards the goals of the PSE programme, the chances of achieving the intended goals are reduced.

The primary school may draw little or no distinction between PSE and other aspects of the curriculum. This can lead to a powerful unity of purpose, but it can also inadvertently lead to important aspects of PSE being overlooked unless they are explicitly identified and articulated before being re-integrated with the rest of the curriculum.

Thacker suggests that the content for PSE is drawn from three sources:

- *individuals and their development;*
- *the class;*
- *the school.*

Geography provides an appropriate context for a number of aspects of these. With regard to aspects of individual development, geography alone is unlikely to throw up many contexts for considering 'the bodily self' and 'the sexual self'. However, the approach chosen for learning in geography can provide contexts for the development of 'the social self' (communication, self presentation, understanding others) and 'the vocational self' (thinking ahead to what kind of citizen to be as an adult, including work, non-work and family issues). Geography can also provide many contexts for the development and consideration of 'the moral/political self', including ideas of right and wrong, and of possible courses of action, for instance in relation to aspects of economic development and environmental issues at scales ranging from the local to the global. In curricular terms geography provides perhaps a unique opportunity to consider the meaning and issues of global citizenship.

But such notions of global citizenship need a firm foundation in immediate experience. Geographical enquiry can explore aspects of the class as a social grouping and in so doing can provide rich contexts for PSE. Examples would include work around ideas of 'where we live' and 'where we come from'; also, surveys of family, friends and neighbours where the results are pooled into a class database, linking the individual, the class and the broader community in ways which are both symbolic and real.

In terms of the school, Thacker identifies a 'set of themes arising from

- *making sense of school;*
- *getting the most out of school as an organisation;*
- *getting the most out of learning;*
- *progressing through school.'* *(pages 262-3)*

Part of 'making sense of school' starts with the school's spatial manifestation - simply, where the different 'bits' are and how they are linked; also, how people in the school utilise the different parts. These are a prerequisite of autonomous spatial behaviour in the school and are as fundamental to any PSE programme as they are to the early development of a sense of place in geography .

Thacker's set of themes leads to two further aspects of learning in PSE, as shown in **Figure 7.4** - learning about onself as a learner, and learning about oneself in relation to the organisational structure of the school.

Self as a learner	**Self in the organisation**
• to reflect on present study strategies;	• to use organisations in constructive ways;
• using others as resources in learning;	• to be an active participant in organisations;
• developing skills of self-assessment;	• to access help in an organisation;
• to engage in group activities for learning;	• to handle transitions between organisations;
• coping with anxiety;	• to make best use of available choices.
• managing time;	
• organising independent work;	Source Thacker (1995, p 263)
• developing a greater range of learning strategies.	

Figure 7.4 Aspects of PSE: the individual and the school

Even a cursory glance at **Figure 7.4** will reveal that many of the processes decribed in this book in relation to teaching and learning in geography are in harmony with several of the aspects of PSE listed here. It is, then, the teacher's educational philosophy and consequent approach to planning for teaching and learning, which determines the opportunities for PSE which will be present in the geography lesson, enabling twin sets of objectives to be tackled. 'Academic knowledge can be rendered interesting and relevant if learning is understood as **a collaborative process rather than a transmission process** and in so doing most of the objectives of PSE could be achieved.' (Brown, 1990, p.47, my emphasis). This view of personal and social education acknowledges that it can be simultaneously both medium and message, in that it both supports 'academic' learning and is a goal in its own right.

Of course, the role of the teacher in this goes beyond simply planning and managing approaches to learning. *How you are as a teacher* is of great significance. There are important qualities which a teacher may display to different degrees (or may not display at all), which can greatly enhance (or, if lacking, inhibit) the processes which are taking place. The psychologist Carl Rogers identifies these attributes as:

- *realness/genuineness as a person, not just a role;*
- *respect for the learner in the form of 'prizing, acceptance and non possessive warmth';*
- *empathic understanding of the student's experiences. (quoted in Thacker, pages 257-8)*

Activity

1. Obtain a copy of your school's policy for PSE/PSD and read it carefully. Discuss and clarify aspects of it if necessary.
2. Attempt to 'map' the links between the geography curriculum and the school's PSE policy.
3. Are there points or aspects of overlap? Are there opportunities for mutual reinforcement? Can you develop your planning for teaching and learning in geography so as to make a genuine simultaneous contribution to PSE/PSD?
4. Clarify your understanding of Rogers' three attributes, perhaps by reading the chapter by Thacker, or by going to the original (Rogers, 1983, pages 122ff). Discuss your understandings with a peer partner.
5. Review your relationships with those you teach in the light of Rogers' three key attributes (above). To what extent are they observable, detectable qualities in your relationships and interactions? You may find it useful to use data from a combination of some of the following: reflection and self-review; video-taping; audio-taping; peer observation.
6. Consider how you can enhance these attributes of 'the teaching you'.

Group work
Fostering true collaborative learning (see main text) is not easy. Much group work has been shown to be learners arranged in groups, yet working as individuals. The benefits of group work only accrue if group processes of discussion, negotiation, clarification, co-operation, sharing and construction of knowledge (see note about constructivism, p.51) are taking place.
*Once again, then, **fitness for purpose** is an important test. Group work is a point on a spectrum of approaches which also includes individual work, paired work and whole class teaching. It is not an end in itself. It is important that, given the range of purposes embraced by your teaching, your students experience a 'rich diet' of appropriately selected strategies. For a more detailed exploration of ideas and issues around group work you are referred to Kerry and Sands (1982).*

Geography and the cross-curricular elements

The 'cross-curricular elements' referred to here and listed in **Figure 7.5** are:

- *cross-curricular skills;*
- *cross-curricular themes;*
- *cross-curricular dimensions.*

CROSS-CURRICULAR THEMES	CROSS-CURRICULAR SKILLS	CROSS-CURRICULAR DIMENSIONS
"The themes have in common the ability to foster discussion of questions of values and belief; they add to knowledge and understanding and they rely on practical activities, decision making, and the inter-relationship of the individual and the community."	*"All these skills are transferable, chiefly independent of content and can be developed in different contexts across the whole curriculum."*	*"A commitment to providing equal opportunities for all pupils, and a recognition that preparation for life in a multicultural society is relevant to all pupils and should permeate every aspect of the curriculum."*
Economic and industrial understanding **Careers education and guidance** **Health education** **Education for citizenship** **Environmental education**	**Communication** **Numeracy** **Study** **Problem solving** **Personal/social** **Information technology**	**Equal opportunities** **Multiculturalism** **Personal and social development** *All quotations are from Curriculum Guidance 3: The Whole Curriculum (1990), NCC*

Figure 7.5 Cross-curricular elements: the National Curriculum Council's view

There are other ways of looking at 'cross-curricularity', and the list in **Figure 7.5**, though extensive, is not exhaustive. Nevertheless, it has gained fairly wide acceptance in schools as a starting point for thinking about other aspects of the 'whole curriculum', and will provide the basis for some comments here. These elements of their classification would, the NCC suggested (NCC, 1990ª), find expression in the curriculum in a number of ways:

- *permeating the whole curriculum;*
- *as part of separately timetabled PSE;*
- *in separately timetabled 'space';*
- *as part of a pastoral/tutorial programme;*
- *as part of 'long block' timetabling arrangement (eg 'sixth day', activity week, timetable suspension).*

Of these, our interest here is particularly with the first in the list, though obviously teachers with a responsibility for or interest in geography will also contribute to the other approaches. Where do the permeating skills, themes and dimensions intersect with geography? As with the previous section in which PSE was the focus, the relationship we are looking for will ideally be reciprocal: what enhancement can these cross curricular elements bring to the geography lesson and what contribution can geography make to their development in return. Even a cursory glance at the list will suggest extensive links.

Permeation: a note of caution
A holistic view of the curriculum would doubtless support the permeation approach, but permeating elements of the curriculum are notoriously difficult to monitor and evaluate. Brown (1990, p.47) feels that experience "of permeation does not necessarily lead one to be optimistic about it. Normally whatever is being permeated just trickles away."

Cross-curricular themes and dimensions

For an exploration of geography's association with four of the the NCC's five themes see Carter and Bailey (1996). For the fifth (careers education), see Fox (1996).

All the NCC's five themes potentially have productive intersections with geography, though the question of precisely what *approach* to take to each of the themes remains to be answered. It will be seen from their titles alone that the themes are open to different interpretation, particularly so in the light of the earlier section on ideologies in education. The series of five guidance booklets (National Curriculum Council, 1990b-f)), each one concentrating on a particular theme, were rather narrowly conceived and, taken together, somewhat Anglo-centric in approach (Marsden 1995, p.160). Since the publication of these booklets as a 'set', others have been 'drip-fed' into the system, (eg National Curriculum Council, 1992; SCAA 1996b).

Cross-curricular themes have had a long association with geography (eg Corney, 1985) and with other 'social subjects': history, RE, sociology, economics etc. This association pre-dates the National Curriculum, and indicates in some cases a wider sense of what constitutes 'cross-curricular' than the National Curriculum Council's five themes. Books by Huckle (1983) and Fien and Gerber (1988) exemplify this trend, examining issues such as welfare, social justice, education for world citizenship, human rights education, peace education and environmental education from an explicitly geographical perspective.

A cross-curricular view of some of the issues around equality in education in the context of the National Curriculum , including a double-page spread on geography's role, can be found in The Runnymede Trust (1993).

Geography's association with the more general cross-curricular dimensions also pre-dates the National Curriculum, (eg Fien and Gerber, 1988; Walford, 1985). Geography continues not only to be informed by an awareness of multiculturalism and equal opportunities, (see, for example, Barrett, 1996) but also to provide a context in which the outcomes of inequalities and prejudice can be studied as spatially manifested phenomena resulting from the operation of spatially contexted processes. Once again it is probably fair to claim that geography is uniquely well-placed to contribute to such aspects of education.

Activity

1. Read your school's policy and/or guidelines on equal opportunities.
2. If your school has an equal opportunities coordinator, arrange to speak to her/him about the policy; if there is a standing committee or working group, arrange to attend some of their meetings.
3. Read the Chapter by Barrett (1996) referred to above.
4. What opportunities are there to develop and enhance the ways in which work in geography supports the equal opportunities policy in your school?
5. Review your own teaching and set yourself targets for development.

Communication as a cross curricular skill

In the same way that geography has a history of explicit engagement with what we now call cross-curricular themes and dimensions, so too have geography teachers examined the relationship between the subject and cross-curricular skills (see **Figure 7.5**). In fact, once one explores the curriculum from a cross-curricular perspective, the potential for connections and overlaps seems almost limitless. Primary school teachers are often particularly good at this sort of whole curriculum thinking, as they tend to live less within a subject-centred world than their secondary counterparts.

I have indicated possibilities for contributing to some of the cross-curricular and **'key skills'** (which also include the application of number, and information technology) elsewhere in this book, so this section will concentrate on one key skill: communication. In 1981 Williams *et al* wrote: "In their geography lessons pupils talk, listen, read, write and think, and so do their teachers. The **language environment** of each classroom is essential to the teaching that goes on...." (p.5) Think about it for a moment. How much of the teaching and learning in geography for which you are responsible could take place in the absence of language? Now ask yourself how far you have attempted to help foster the development of language, both as a means to an end in learning geography and as a key skill for life and learning in its own right.

In the late 1970s the *Language Across the Curriculum Project* (quoted by Slater, 1982, p.112) identified what they felt were three main types of writing (which apply to talk as well), reflecting three underlying purposes:

*   **transactional** writing, in which the purpose is to 'get things done', eg by instructing, explaining, informing and persuading; formal in style, often used to classify and record information;
*   **expressive** (more appropriately **'exploratory'**) writing, which is 'thinking aloud on paper';
*   **poetic** writing, which shapes language for its own sake.

Studies had revealed a preponderance of transactional writing in geography (one project, *The Schools Council Writing Across the Curriculum Project*, put the figure at 88%) (Molyneux and Tolley, 1987, p.37). The conclusion was that more expressive/exploratory writing was needed in order to support and enhance the process of making meaning through the use of language in geography. Better still, **discussion** of an exploratory nature occurring around collaborative activities would enable meaning to be constructed in the manner identified and described in Vygotsky's 'constructivist' approach. (see p. 51, including margin note)

In order to provide for language development in geography through the learning activities you plan it is worth remembering the simple dictum 'vary the **audience**, vary the function'. (Slater, 1989, p.12) This should help you to build language development explicitly into your planning by thinking about the role of audience in the learning activities which comprise your teaching of geography, but remember that 'audiences should be realistic and plausible' (Butt, 1996, p.193). Remenber too that as Butt points out, very often 'teacher as assessor' will be the perceived audience for written work. The twin concepts of audience and language **register** have been given additional emphasis in the National Curriculum for English, but they permeate work in a range of subjects, including geography.

Consider the different language demands implicit in these two instructions: "discuss with your partner what happened in the Mississippi floods," and "with your partner write a newspaper front page about the Mississippi floods for display at open day". In the first instruction the use of language is oral only and the audience is restricted to self and partner, a fellow student. Informal and exploratory use of language will probably ensue. The discussion is largely private and therefore 'safe'.

In the second task exploratory discussion will probably again take place, but there will also be transactional oral use of language in organising who is going to do which parts of the task. The newspaper front page will require that transactional written language is used in a particular way (register) and following certain conventions appropriate to the **genre** (for instance the use of alliteration and the suspension of some of the rules of sentence construction in a 'punchy'

Language development and geography
Note that not only is it good practice for you to foster language development intentionally through your geography teaching - it is now also statutory, as a common requirement of the National Curriculum programmes of study. "Pupils should be taught to express themselves clearly in both speech and writing, and to develop their reading skills. They should be taught to use gramatically correct sentences and to spell and punctuate accurately in order to communicate effectively in written English." (DFE, 1995, p. 1)

The fostering and management of purposeful discussion is an important teaching skill. One still hears the comment "we had a good discussion" when what is meant is "I asked some closed questions and members of an otherwise silent class put up their hands and gave the right answers". There is of course a place for this, but student learning through talk as a process requires very careful planning and management if the talk is to be productive. As will be seen (pages 78-79) discussion is a vital aspect of the development of thinking skills.

Drafting and wordprocessing
When IT is being used to support writing, it is preferable for the **whole drafting process to take place using the computer,** *otherwise the benefits of on-screen editing and manipulation of text are not experienced. Children who are reluctant to re-draft hand-written work because of the effort involved, can be more critical of work on screen and can alter it more easily.*

Further, this aspect of IT capability is not developed if hand-drafted work is brought to the computer to be 'typed up neatly'. This is nothing more than an exercise in presentation.

Group writing through discussion is easier as several individuals can see the screen simultaneously.

It is not hard to see how four sets of objectives covering aspects of:

- *geography;*
- *language development;*
- *IT capability;*
- *personal and social development could be covered simultaneously in work of this sort.*

headline - eg 'Flood fear as Mississippi bursts banks!'). **Drafting**, a process which here moves the user from exploratory written language to transactional written language will probably be needed. In terms of audience for the writing, there is an imaginary newspaper readership, but the true audience is the teacher and the parents and visitors on open day.

This simple (!) example indicates that it is very important to be aware of the language demands of the work you plan. The most reliable way of achieving this is to have objectives in the form of learning outcomes for language development as well as for geography. The example also indicates that the kind of preparation, 'pre-teaching' and support which you will provide as teacher again depends upon the language demands of the task you set, as well as the geographical demands. For instance, in the above example productive drafting is unlikely to occur spontaneously (unless, of course, your students have already learnt how and why to do it and it has become a natural part of the writing process for them - see **Figure 7.6**).

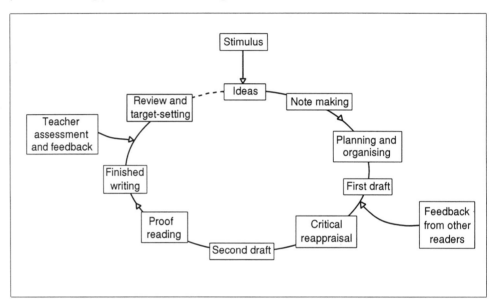

Figure 7.6 The drafting cycle

Activity

1. Review your recent geography teaching for the language demands and development which are embedded in it, both explicit and implicit. You may find it helpful to concentrate on a week's teaching, or a sequence of work with one class.
2. Refer to the National Curriculum Order for English, for the key stage in which you are working. Are the language demands and development embedded in your teaching of geography consistent with the relevant National Curriculum programme of study for English?
3. Arrange to discuss the way in which you are approaching the use and development of language in your teaching of geography with your school's English coordinator or Head of English department.
4. Read the article on 'audience-centred' teaching and children's writing by Butt (1996).
5. Set yourself appropriate targets for developing your own approach to the use and development of language through your teaching of geography.

The language of geography
Not only does geography make a contribution to language development - it has its own subject terminology which should be acquired and then used appropriately. One way of focusing on this is for you to do as follows:

- *Review your schemes of work for such terminology (look out too for where particular use is made in geography of a word which also has other meanings in other contexts).*
- *Encourage your students, as they encounter these words, to build up progressively their own glossary.*
- *Check for their accurate and appropriate use of the words in discussion and written work.*

Thinking as a cross-curricular skill

What do all the following have in common?

- *the accurate striking of a lob in tennis;*
- *the aesthetic appreciation of a piece of pottery;*
- *judging the reliability of items of historical evidence;*
- *empathising with Masai herdspeople as they come to terms with modern tourism;*
- *writing a poem;*
- *solving simultaneous equations.*

Of course they all, along with too many other activities to mention, involve thinking. Thinking is a process which is as fundamental to education as it is to life. As a word it has a non-threatening, 'everyday' feel to it. But one does not often find it in the index of books about education and teaching. Perhaps it is just too large a term, too vague and too difficult to pin down. 'Cognitive development', on the other hand, appears slightly more often in such indexes, but has overtones of educational psychology and perhaps feels too specialised for everyday use. Certainly one does not often hear it in the staffroom, and less than that in the classroom. Yet "What are you doing, Gary?" "Thinking, Miss," has a familiar ring to it, as does the exasperated staffroom observation, "You know, 7Q just won't **think** about their work."

One could argue that to improve children's ability to think (or, if you like, enhance their cognitive development) across a range of purposes such as those which began this Section is so fundamental a goal in education that we should all be thinking about it, and doing something about it, for more of the time than we are.

This is something of a mis-representation. In fact we are 'doing something about it' for much of the time, without necessarily making our intentions explicit as regards the larger picture of cognitive development. The learning objectives which we identify often involve thinking in some way or another. as we can see if we remind ourselves of the three domains of Bloom's taxonomy which underlie much of our planning for intended learning outcomes:

- *cognitive domain (knowing, understanding, reasoning, evaluating);*
- *affective domain (attitudes and values);*
- *psychomotor domain (physical skills).*

The cognitive domain is, of course, all about thinking, (but see de Bono's fallacies, below). Cognitive development is also heavily involved in the educational concepts of differentiation, continuity and progression, and underlies the concept of levels in the National Curriculum, though as Adey and Shayer (1994, p.10) point out, the raising of standards is not achieved simply by establishing in law *what* young people should learn. "It is *how* they learn it that matters."

Perhaps one of the reasons why the explicit rôle of thinking in all of this remains rather shadowy is because at the heart lies a paradox, or at least a tension. Schools are sites of cultural reproduction; indeed, this could be said to be their primary purpose. Society needs young people to be schooled to take their place in that society. This is a profoundly conservative process in that, by definition, it is antithetical to social change. Yet increasing young people's powers to think autonomously, a true educational goal, runs the risk of putting them beyond the cultural reproductive process as it gives them the power to question and critically analyse the very culture which is being reproduced through the experience of schooling.

In his keynote presentation to the 1989 Conference of the Organisation for Economic Cooperation and Development, Edward de Bono noted that all educational systems will claim to teach thinking skills because it is such a fundamental aim that "no educator could possibly admit that it is not already happening". (de Bono, 1991, p.3) He pointed out four fallacies which underlie the false assumption that the teaching of thinking is, in fact, taking place.

The four fallacies about the teaching of thinking which de Bono identified were:
- **Intelligence is the same as thinking skills.** *It is not. Intelligent people can be poor thinkers. Intelligence is potential which requires thinking skills in order to be used effectively.*
- **Teaching knowledge is sufficient.** *There is too much knowledge to teach it all, and the knowledge explosion is only just beginning. Thinking skills are necessary to access, sort and use knowledge effectively, and to develop new knowledge.*
- **Thinking skills are taught within every subject.** *Some are being taught implicitly, but these tend to be low-order and fall short of what is needed for life and for development.*
- **Any thinking that is taking place will develop better thinking skills.** *Merely practising a skill simply re-inforces existing habits - it is not of itself developmental. (de Bono, p.4)*

The knowledge explosion has yet to happen! A group of American researchers has predicted that we currently know just 1% of what we will know by the year 2050!

In the debate around the raising of educational standards, attention has begun to focus on the rôle of thinking, and through this on the process of teaching young people to think. Experience from the Cognitive Acceleration through Science Education (CASE) project has been encouraging,

Instrumental Enrichment

Much of the content of current approaches to teaching thinking is based on the pioneering work of the Israeli psychologist Reuven Feuerstein. His approach of instrumental enrichment was originally developed for less able and disadvantaged learners, but a wider application of the ideas has proved to be possible.

providing empirical evidence to support those who *"reject the idea of intelligence as a fixed potential and who believe that educational intervention rooted in well-established theories of cognitive development can have long-term and replicable effects on young adolescents' academic achievement."* (Adey and Shayer)

The purpose of 'thinking skills programmes' is to support students in tackling demanding work. 'Rather than 'water down' the curriculum to improve the student's chance of success, the aim is to develop the student's ability to cope with intellectually challenging tasks, leading to improved self esteem through genuine achievement.' (Tyneside TEC/Newcastle University, 1995, p.3)

The rôle of the teacher in this is that of **mediator** working with learners to provide social support to enable them to make the gains in understanding identified by Vygotsky as lying within their zone of proximal development. (see page 51) This is achieved through what is essentially a simple process, though calling for sophisticated skills on the part of the teacher:

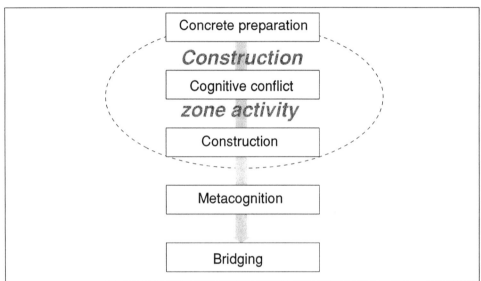

Figure 7.7 Five key elements of cognitive acceleration

In the model given in **Figure 7.7**, the elements are as follows:

- *concrete preparation involves introducing new vocabulary and includes getting the learners confident in its use;*
- *cognitive conflict involves an activity in which what is observed does not fit with learners' pre-existing mental framework; "a puzzle which is interesting and attackable." (Adey and Shayer, p.75) Resolution must be within the learners' reach, but must force alteration of the mental framework;*
- *construction zone activity involves reasoning to resolve the cognitive conflict through discussion, in the process of which "students' minds go beyond their previous thinking capability." (Adey and Shayer)*
- *metacognition (thinking about thinking) involves conscious reflection on, articulation and naming through discussion of the thinking and reasoning processes used to handle the problem;*
- *bridging is the linking through discussion of the thinking so identified to other situations in order to generalise and consolidate the learning.*

We can see that the teacher has a very important part to play in planning and preparing, in being fairly 'hands-off' during the construction zone activity (or judging the right moment to introduce the cognitive conflict), and in probing and leading during the metacognition and bridging which constitute the activity's de-briefing. The important thing to note is that focus of the planning is on how the entire sequence will extend the learners' thinking, rather than how best to tell them about something. "There is a deep-rooted desire within people to exercise their minds. What we need in the whole school curriculum, for all abilities, is to release and capitalise on this desire, rather than to bottle, channel and eventually to kill it." (Adey, 1991, p.91)

Activity

1. If you are interested in the ideas you have encountered in this short section you may like to take your thinking further. One way of doing this is to write to the 'Thinking Through Geography Group', David Leat, Department of Education, University of Newcastle, Newcastle upon Tyne, NE1 7RU.

Critical thinking

"Democracies need people who know their own minds, and teachers who can promote responsible learning."

Desforges, 1995, p.7

We have already seen elsewhere in this book that geography is best approached in a questioning, inquiring manner. This is an aspect of what might be termed 'critical thinking', itself a set of cognitive tools for examining what passes for knowledge. Critical thinking is thus a form of procedural knowledge, ie 'know-how' (Bresson, 1991, p.174), involving metaknowledge (knowledge about knowledge - whose it is, how it is made etc.). Thus one who is able to engage in critical thinking will, when faced with a problem or body of knowlege in geography, be able to:

*   *identify issues central to the matter in hand;*
*   *recognise and confront underlying values, assumptions and ideologies;*
*   *evaluate evidence for, or authority of, knowledge as propositions (including relevance, bias, emotionality, verifiability);*
*   *maintain a stance of curiosity and constructive scepticism;*
*   *draw her/his own conclusions.*

You will have noticed that these are close to some of the aspects of autonomy referred to earlier (page 50). You will also have recognised that these dispositions and abilities do not occur spontaneously. Their development among young people can be fostered, or it can be suppressed, according to the way in which you approach your teaching. Postman and Weingartner (1971, p.16), quoting a pithy remark from Ernest Hemingway, describe the disposition towards critical thinking as a 'crap detector'. The development of this in each young person is, they argue, the particular responsibility of teachers, as others lack either the opportunity, having insufficient access to young people, or the motivation, having a vested interest in not being subjected to critical scrutiny (p.25).

This is not just unreconstructed 60s radicalism. Most schools have in their aims something along the lines of "to help young people develop lively and enquiring minds, the ability to question and argue rationally...". If this is not to be empty rhetoric, it means critical thinking. (The quotation, incidentally, is from the Department of Education and Science's aims for the curriculum in *The School Curriculum,* 1981, quoted by Marsden, 1995, p.9)

There are therefore clear and important implications for how you as teacher see your rôle. Lists of competences may have their place, but they also carry implicit messages about the teacher's rôle, not least that it can be defined by others. But suppose we problematise this. Will you define your own rôle or have it defined for you? Will you encourage critical thinking and, if so, how? Do you want to foster autonomy through your teaching? Where will you stand on the matter of 'neutrality'? Stenhouse in the Humanities Curriculum Project felt that it was essential for the teacher to adopt a neutral, chairing rôle where discussion of values was concerned. By contrast, "teachers are bound to operate within the framework of the economic, political, social and cultural realities of which the education system is only a part, but it is not a requirement of education to preserve a status quo of social inequality..... to remain 'neutral' is to condone the inequality of society rather than to challenge it." (Roberts, 1986, p.84)

Thus the writers of *Teaching Geography for a Better World* (Fien and Gerber,1988) explicitly recognised their underlying values in what they termed 'a socially critical geography' to include:

*   *"the promotion of social justice, participatory democracy, respect for human rights and ecological sustainability as the values base for society;*

Critical thinking, social justice and human rights education

"...a critical, self-actualizing pedagogy, building the habits of critical reflection and democratic discussion, is clearly implied in any programme grounded in social justice. Creating democratic people for life in just communities should take place in environments where learner autonomy, openness, co-operation and civility are prized above deference and unquestioning conformity:

> *Democracy is best learned in a democratic setting where participation is encouraged, where views can be expressed openly and discussed, where there is freedom of expression for pupils and teachers and where there is fairness and justice. An appropriate climate is, therefore, an essential complement to learning about human rights."*
> *Council of Europe, 1985, Appendix 4.1.*
> *(Steiner, 1996, p.198)*

A commitment to critical thinking involves the development of a range of 'literacies' in order that students can 'read' the world around them and recognise the way in which discourses are constructed and manipulated.

Particularly significant in this context are:

*   *political literacy (see, for instance, Huckle, J 'Political Education' in Huckle, 1983, pages 82 - 88);*
*   *media literacy (see, for instance, Clarke, M 'Media Education: Critical times?' in Dufour, 1990, pages 69 - 82)*

- *the development of an analysis that identifies the inequities and problems resulting fro the often taken-for-granted social structures and processes that contradict these values;*
- *the development of the insights and skills necessary to question such structures and processes, evaluate them according to principles of social justice, democracy, human rights and ecological sustainability and, in particular to ask questions about the power relationships involved and about who gains and who loses from any decision or change in the social system;*
- *the development of a willingness and the skills to propose alternative patterns, solutions and futures, and to work with others to help bring about a more just, democratic and ecologically sustainable world at local, national and global levels." (p.8)*

Activity

*You may find it interesting to look at the profile Figure 1.1 in **Beginning Teaching Workbook 6**. Based on the Northern Ireland profile, it contains an explicit statement of professional values.*

1. The above statement of values from *Teaching Geography for a Better World* amounts to a 'manifesto' or 'mission statement' for geography teaching of a particular sort. Read it again. With how much of it do you agree and/or disagree?

2. Look back at the table of descriptions of ideologies. Which is closest to the position adopted by *Teaching Geography for a Better World*?

3. Think about the question 'what is the purpose of school geography?' What answer can you give to this question?

4. Write your own manifesto for the teaching of geography. Note that it should contain the values you actually hold personally and which inform your approach. (These may of course differ from the position adopted by your department or school.)

5. How much of your teaching of geography reflects the values of your personal manifesto?

8

To be continued ....

"Who controls the past controls the future. Who controls the present controls the past."

George Orwell, 'Nineteen Eighty-Four'

Aims

What is 'to be continued ....'? A geographical enquiry being undertaken by some students? A piece of action research you are conducting? Your professional development? The development of geography as a subject? Change in education? The lives of the young people you teach? Technological, social, political and economic change? Bruner's 'unfinished business of man's (*sic*) evolution'? (1967, p.101) Yes, all of these, and more, are to be continued .....

One of the underlying aims of this book has been to encourage you to seek to exercise participative autonomy in your professional life as a teacher, and to foster it in those whom you teach. Through much of the book the future has been an implicit presence, an indistinct, unmapped territory into which your professional development will take you, and into which the learning and growth of those whom you teach will take them. In this last Chapter our attention turns explicitly to that future. In particular, I shall concentrate on two aspects:

* *teaching about the future;*
* *your professional future as a teacher.*

Both of these, as we shall see, incorporate ideas of participative autonomy.

Teaching about the future

At first sight teaching about the future might seem to be a ridiculous proposition, certainly from the 'teaching as telling' perspective. The future by definition is unknown, so cannot be taught about in the same way as those things which are thought of as established factual knowledge. Perhaps this is one reason why teaching about the future is neglected - positivism finds it problematic, being beyond objective verification other than 'wait and see'. So how should we regard the future in education in general and in geography in particular?

There is no doubt that the future plays an enormous rôle in the present. "Today is yesterday's tomorrow" was a popular slogan in the 1960s (and may be again, one day). Our perception of the future, both short- and long-term, has a profound influence on our current actions and choices.

> *"Images of the future play a central rôle in social and cultural change at both personal and societal levels. It is important to know about people's hopes and fears for the future because they influence what individuals and groups are prepared to do, or not do, in the present."*
>
> *Hicks and Holden, 1995, p.4*

The future can thus be seen to influence the geography of the present, by influencing the values and perceptions of decision makers.

A broad aim of education is to prepare young people for the future. For instance, the Education Reform Act of 1988 requires a curriculum which:

> *"promotes the spiritual, moral, cultural, mental and physical development of pupils at the school and of society;*
>
> *prepares such pupils for the opportunities, responsibilities and experiences of adult life."*

The future is implied in the 'development' of the first clause and rather more heavily implied ('pupils' as future 'adults') in the second. However both clauses are instances of what Gough (see margin note) calls 'tacit futures'.

Images of the future in Western society of the late twentieth century are often pessimistic, pointing to something worse than today (Hicks and Holden). This vision is reinforced by news of crime, wars and disasters, and by dystopian fiction ('*Brave New World*', '*The Handmaid's Tale*', '*Stark*') and film ('*Rollerball*', '*Mad Max*', '*Bladerunner*'). It is also reinforced by suggestions that

*Gough, quoted in Hicks and Holden (1995, pages 14 - 15) analysed a range of education documents to see how they dealt with the future. Overall he found that the future was conspicuous by its absence from explicit mention, whereas the past and the present figured strongly. He called this **temporal asymmetry**. However, the future is present in educational writing through implicit reference. There are three levels of this:*

* *tacit futures are quite deeply buried and may only be apparent to the practised eye;*
* *token futures are more explicit, but tend to be limited to rhetorical references, eg 'education for the future'. The future element is not clarified or developed;*
* *taken-for-granted futures are presented as a fact, a fait accompli. A particular future will be presented unproblematically, without alternatives, eg continued economic growth to provide rising standards of living.*

*(See also **Figure 8.1**)*

'things' (eg teaching approaches, moral values) were better in previous times and need to be returned to. Widely-held negative images of the future may indicate a society in decline, with quite literally nothing to look forward to. The danger is that this legitimates an 'opting out' into individualism, away from social responsibility and democratic participation. It may also prevent those with a claim on the future from exercising that claim, leaving the way open for others to construct and colonise the future their way, eg the violent, sexist, technocentric futures of the computer game manufacturers.

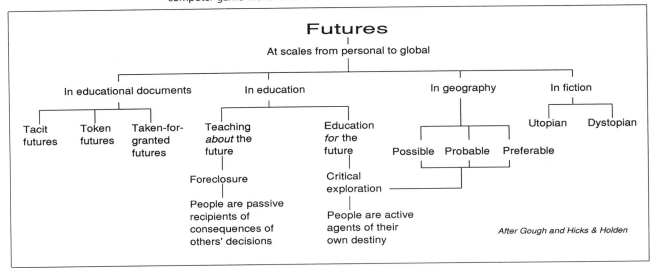

Figure 8.1 Futures - a possible classification

So "the future", as L P Hartley might have said, "is a foreign country: they will do things differently there." How differently? Why differently? Who says so, and why? Who will benefit and who will not? Can we have an influence? We can see from such questions that the sort of critical thinking described at the end of Chapter 7 can have a rôle in explorations of the future.

These explorations can take the form of a geographical enquiry, either in the late stages of an enquiry or as a starting point for an enquiry into geographical futures. They key question in this context would be 'what will/may happen next?' which in turn leads to further questions (**Figure 8.2**). This underlies the emphasis in geography on understanding process, and its relationship with 'pattern' (ie spatial outcome). We can see from **Figure 8.1** that this will lead us to consider:

- **possible futures**, *ie those which can be envisaged;*
- **probable futures**, *ie those which are most likely to come about;*
- **preferable futures**, *ie those which reflect our hopes, wishes and values.*

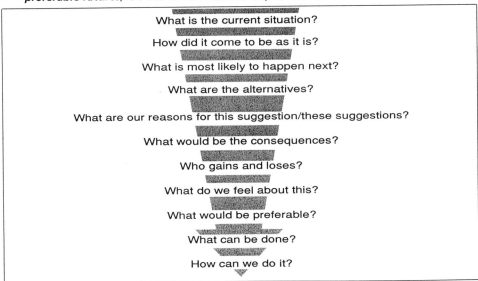

Figure 8.2 A possible 'futures enquiry' route in geography

The title given to this section of this Chapter was, provocatively, 'teaching *about* the future'. As Hicks and Holden (p.10) point out, this description is neither desirable nor appropriate. They argue that to achieve a more just and ecologically sustainable future and to empower young people to play their part in creating it requires an explicitly *pro-future,* transformative stance on the part of the teacher, hence their preferred description, 'education *for* the future'.

In geography this is of considerable relevance to the theme of **environment** and, in particular, of **environmental sustainability**, which can be seen as rational explorations of the future of humankind and nature in an interdependent world. (Interestingly, in the current National Curriculum Order for geography in England and Wales (DFE 1995), though the terms 'sustainable development', 'environmental change', 'stewardship', 'conservation', 'environmental planning' and 'proposed changes' all occur, the word 'future' does not - a clear case of Gough's 'tacit futures'.) Nevertheless, geography itself has a record of explicitly addressing the future, eg *Geographical Futures* (King, 1985) as well as as its own future as a subject, eg *The Future of Geography* (Johnston, 1985).

It is appropriate then, that some real responsibility for, and commitment to, education for the future should mark out geography as one of the growth points of the emerging field of **education for sustainability.** This new field draws together aspects of environmental education, development education, peace education, world studies and human rights education in a framework informed by a critical approach to the theory and practice of education. It recognises the nine principles of a Sustainable Society identified in *Caring for the Earth: A Strategy for Sustainable Living* (IUCN, UNEP, WWF, 1991) and examines the way in which education can contribute to a future in which the people of the Earth can live harmoniously with one another and with the small planet which is home.

This of course has implications not only for the content of the curriculum, but also for the practices of the school. "Pupils' learning is likely to be most effective where curriculum content is matched by the school's own environmental practices..." (SCAA, 1996[b] p.5) It also has implications for the approaches to be chosen towards teaching and learning, particularly if your aim is to "arouse pupils' awareness and curiosity about the environment and *encourage active participation in resolving environment problems.*" (DfEE/DOE, 1995, in SCAA, 1996[b] p.2, my emphasis.) Several of the threads in this book concerning learner-centred approaches, democracy, autonomy, participation, critical thinking and enquiry come together in this pedagogy. This is as much a matter for you in your rôle as a self-empowering, autonomous, collaborative professional as it is for your approach towards those whom you teach. It marks out the territory in which you can stand with your colleagues and your students as partners in 'the learning school'.

Activity

1. Read some items from the short reading list in the margin in order to develop your knowlededge and understanding about environmental education.
2. Research your school's policy on environmental education:
   - Is there one and, if so, when was it written and/or revised?
   - Who is responsible for implementation, monitoring and evaluation in the school?
   - Talk to the school's co-ordinator for environmental education. What is her/his perception of the way the school approaches environmental education?
3. Consider some of your teaching which is in the planning stage:
   - Can you introduce more of the content of environmental education?
   - Are your teaching approaches consistent with the messages you want to get across about attitudes and values and the participative skills you intend to develop?
   - Plan and teach the lessons with enhanced attention paid to aspects of environmental education/education for sustainability.
   - If possible, arrange for the school's coordinator for environmental education to observe some of your work and/or hold a review and evaluation discussion with you.
4. If you are interested in taking your thinking about environmental education and education for sustainability further, contact: *Reaching Out, Teacher Education, WWF UK, Panda House, Weyside Park, Godalming, Surrey GU7 1XR (Tel: 01483 426444).*

For a very readable, thought-provoking account of some possible futures for geography, see Walford and Haggett. (1995)

The Nine Principles of a Sustainable Society
- *Respect and care for the community of life*
- *Improve the quality of life*
- *Conserve the Earth's vitality and diversity*
- *Minimise the depletion of non-renewable resources*
- *Keep within the Earth's carrying capacity*
- *Change personal attitudes and practices*
- *Enable communities to care for their own environments*
- *Provide a national framework for integrating development and conservation*
- *Create a global alliance*

(From Caring for the Earth: A Strategy for Sustainable Living)

Environmental education: further reading
- *Greig, S, Pike, G and Selby, D (1987) Earthrights: Education as if the Planet Really Mattered*
- *Greig, S, Pike, G and Selby, D (1989) Greenprints for changing schools*
- *Huckle, J (1990) 'Environmental Education: teaching for a sustainable future' in Dufour, B The New Social Curriculum,*
- *Palmer, J and Neal, P (1994) The Handbook of Environmental Education,*
- *SCAA (1996) Teaching Environmental Matters through the National Curriculum*
- *Woods, P (1995) Creative Teachers in Primary Schools (Chapter 3)*
- *WWF UK (1994) Let's Reach Out Handbook (Primary)*
- *WWF UK (1994) Let's Reach Out Handbook (Secondary)*

To be continued .....

Your professional future

If you have done all the activities signposted in this book and drawn as appropriate on its companion volumes in the *Beginning Teaching Workbooks* series, you should have laid a very secure foundation for your on-going professional development as a teacher of geography. In this final section of the book we will take stock of your development to date and review some of the possibilities for sustaining and extending the forward momentum of your development. This is important, as there is an old adage in teaching that you can have ten years' experience or one year's experience repeated ten times. This book is based on an assumption that you wish to be in the former category!

Hancock and Settle (1990) suggest that there are two underlying questions any teacher should have in mind when undertaking 'self evaluation':

- *'what aspects of current performance do I need to improve?*
- *what new skills do I need to equip myself with, and what new knowledge do I need, whether for improvement in my present post or for a future move?' (p.30)*

The quick self-review (**Figure 8.3**) of some of the aspects covered in this book complements some of the self analysis of more general aspects of your teaching competences which are covered in the *Beginning Teaching Workbooks.* Together they should provide you with some data to help you answer the above two questions. Any list such as that in **Figure 8.3** reads like a 'counsel of perfection', and there is no suggestion being made here that to do all that is in the list effectively is easy! The list contains the elements of a long-term, on-going process, and in truth most of us have to continue to develop and work on aspects of the list throughout our careers in our attempt to improve the quality of what we do.

Activity

1. Complete the self-review grid (you may find it preferable to make a photocopy).
2. Set targets for development as appropriate. You may find you need more space for targets, in which case use a continuation sheet and insert codes in the final column. In setting targets remember to make them 'S M A R T', ie:
   - **S**pecific
   - **M**anageable
   - **A**chievable
   - **R**elevant
   - **T**ime-related
3. Date the review sheet and store it in your professional development portfolio.
   There will be other aspects of competence, perhaps more generic (eg management of discussion; questioning skills; use of rewards and sanctions) and identified via some other profiling instrument, which you will wish to develop alongside whatever targets you set here. Bear this in mind, particularly with regard to manageability.
4. You may find it appropriate to conduct the above process through a development dialogue, perhaps with a mentor or some one else with an oversight of your professional development. An alternative is to work with a peer partner.
5. Some of your targets will have resource implications, eg you may feel you need to attend a course or conference related to an area you have identified for further development. In this case you should talk to your mentor / head of department / subject leader to seek their approval and then approach your school's staff development co-ordinator with your plans.

Development activities

The list of development activities (p. 86) may help trigger some thoughts about ways you can take your development forward in your school. Some of them are appropriate whether or not you have already qualified, whereas others will only be appropriate if you have been working as a teacher for at least a year or two. The list is based on a section of *Professional Development in School.* (Dean, 1991, pages 21 - 25)

Self-review statements	Strongly applies to me	Applies to me intermittently	I'd like this to apply more to me	Not an area I wish to pursue	Target, action or comment
• I understand the purpose of teaching geography and can articulate geography's contribution to the curriculum to students, colleagues, parents and governors, as appropriate.					
• I am fully familiar with all relevant National Curriculum and syllabus requirements for geography, for the age groups I teach.					
• My planning for geography identifies clearly the intended learning outcomes.					
• My teaching of geography integrates the three key elements of skills, themes and places.					
• Through my teaching, my students are gaining a better knowledge and understanding of a variety of places, from the local and familiar to the distant and unfamiliar.					
• My geography teaching ranges across scales from the local to the global.					
• I guard against stereotyping, bias, and ethnocentrism in my teaching about place, development and other issues.					
• Enquiry is central to the way I teach geography.					
• I successfully integrate a wide range of learning resources into my geography teaching.					
• I successfully foster a sense of place in those I teach.					
• I provide for first-hand experience through fieldwork wherever possible.					
• I successfully integrate the use of information technology into my geography teaching.					
• I use a variety of approaches to teaching and learning in geography, with an emphasis on active learning approaches.					
• I plan a variety of approaches to assessment into my geography teaching and see assessment as an integral, continuous process.					
• I actively explore and forge links between geography and other subjetcs.					
• I recognise and provide for the personal and social education and development of young people through my geography teaching.					
• I actively investigate and provide for a contribution to the cross-curricular skills themes and dimensions from the perspective of geography.					
• I recognise and provide for the opportunity to develop language and communication skills, including speaking and listening, and reading and writing, through my teaching of geography.					
• I recognise and provide for the opportunity to develop thinking skills, including critical thinking, through my teaching of geography.					
• I recognise and provide for the opportunities to identify, explore and discuss alternative futures in my teaching of geography.					
• I have networks and access to information which keep me abreast of change in the subject and in the world, enabling my teaching to reflect this in its relevance.					

Figure 8.3 A self-review profile for reflectively investigating your development as a teacher of geography

See also Chapter 1 'Furthering your professional development' in Beginning Teaching Workbook 6 (Tolley et al, 1996)

A list of possible development activities:

- *acting as a voluntary deputy (eg to your subject leader or head of department);*
- *action research (see page 6);*
- *coaching (a more experienced colleague may coach you in a particular skill, or you may offer coaching to colleagues in an area in which you are proficient and they wish to develop);*
- *experimental work in the teaching situation (especially if you can pair with a colleague);*
- *giving a talk to a group of colleagues, parents or governors;*
- *keeping a diary or reflective journal;*
- *observation (both of and by you) and discussion;*
- *personal reading and study (this can be greatly enhanced by tying it in to a sequence of discussions/seminars with colleagues);*
- *preparing a report from reading or of an investigation;*
- *structured reflection and self-review;*
- *shadowing a colleague;*
- *taking on responsibility and getting involved in decision-making;*
- *joining a task or working group or committee and/or working with other teachers;*
- *teaching a variety of groups;*
- *triangulation of perspectives on a lesson: teacher, observer, learners;*
- *visiting other schools to see alternatives and provide a context for reflection (particularly beneficial if collaborative, enabling discussion about shared experiences).*

Development partners

The introduction to this book included some comments about your development as an autonomous, collaborative professional. Initially much of your collaboration may well have been with people from two groups:

- *those 'in the same boat' as you, eg fellow students / NQTs (including specific peer partners);*
- *those with a direct responsibilty for you, eg, tutors, mentors etc.*

This will probably have provided a basis for a broader network of collegial relationships as you have become more established. You may also be broadening your network further to include parents and governors. Assuming that you are 'established' in this way you may wish to exercise your autonomy by seeking further extension of your network by developing other partnerships, perhaps with specific foci or with specific purposes in mind. Some of the possibilities for developmental partnerships beyond your school are:

- *the local branch of the Geographical Association;*
- *LEA advisory and inspection staff, eg for geography, environmental education etc;*
- *LEA advisory teachers;*
- *teachers in other schools, eg members of your local cluster of schools, including same-phase and 'cross-phase' parnerships;*
- *local teacher-led consortia for curriculum development around new syllabuses;*
- *local training and enterprise council (TEC);*
- *local business and industry, eg for visits, guest speakers etc;*
- *a higher education institution involved in teacher training (possibilities include consultancy, networking, library facilities, mentor training, accreditation of prior experiential learning (APEL) schemes, higher degrees etc);*
- *local voluntary sector organisations, eg your county wildlife trust, local branch of the British Trust for Conservation Volunteers or Groundwork Trust;*
- *your local development education centre (DEC);*
- *field centres and urban studies centres.*

Postscript: your teaching doughnut

A margin note in Chapter 3 introduced Charles Handy's doughnut principle. (If you did not read the note, do so now.) This is probably a good time for you to take stock, to examine your personal doughnut. Not at this stage your entire personal doughnut, but your personal teaching doughnut. Whether you are a student or an NQT, you will be able to identify your 'core', the things you must do as your professional duty. Some of this core will involve the teaching of geography.

But there will also be the outer ring of other things related to your work in teaching which you feel you ought to do, or wish to do for personal development. Perhaps there are other things which are simply for job satisfaction or plain enjoyment. Some of them may or may not relate to the teaching of geography.

Activity

1. Use **Figure 8.4** to identify core and discretionary elements of your teaching doughnut.

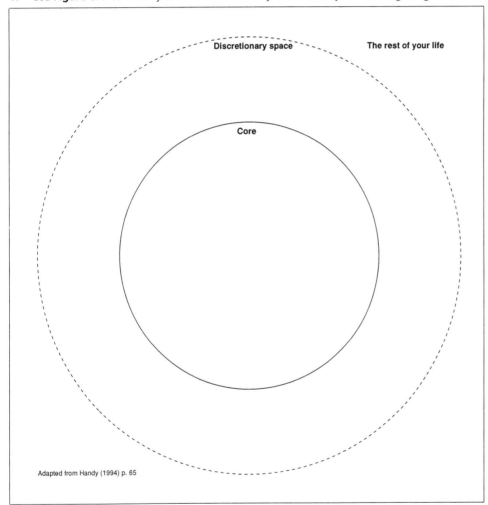

Figure 8.4 appears with labels "Discretionary space", "The rest of your life", and "Core".

*In **The Empty Raincoat** Handy describes a job which was "...all core and no space. That way the organisation got no surprises, or so it hoped. All was predictable, planned and controlled. It was also dull and frustrating, with no space for self-expression, no space to make a difference, no empowerment."*
He also describes the danger of the boundless doughnut "Without a boundary it is easy to be oppressed by guilt, for enough is never enough...... A sensible job is a balanced doughnut." (Handy, p.68)

Adapted from Handy (1994) p. 65

Figure 8.4 Your teaching 'doughnut'

2. This personal audit of 'you-as-teacher' may have been revealing.
   - If your 'core' is too big in relation to the whole doughnut you may need to reappraise your situation. If you have no freedom, no flexibility, only obligations in your work, how long will it be before you find it unfulfilling, or even come to resent it?
   - If your teaching doughnut is too big overall, what implications does this have for other aspects of your professional and personal life?
   - If your teaching doughnut is too small overall, you may feel that you need to take on some additional responsibilities.

3. You may wish to discuss the results of this audit with someone with whom you feel comfortable. This might be a peer partner or friend, but could equally be someone with a designated responsibility for your professional wellbeing, eg a professional tutor or mentor.

4. If the results of this analysis indicate a need for some sort of change, eg an extension of the discretionary element to balance the core, or a reduction in the size of the discretionary element to avoid early burn out, formulate an action plan to tackle the situation. Identify:
   - what you are going to do;
   - others who may be important in the process;
   - the date by which you will have achieved your goal.

5. Now identify:
   - the factors which may assist you to achieve your goal, and how you can maximise their effects;
   - the factors which may inhibit you in achieving your goal, and how you can minimise their effect.

Do not treat this activity as a one-off. Make it an ongoing part of how you review your work. As you change and develop, and as your responsibilities within and beyond the job change, so does the doughnut.

Some years before Charles Handy had written about the doughnut principle, Robin Richardson in the book *Geographical Education: Reflection and Action* (Huckle, 1983) wrote:

> "**Acknowledging oneself as a teacher**
>
> *A teacher who reads and sympathises with the other chapters in this book (ie Huckle, 1983) and intends to act on them, or to continue acting on them, is likely to be able to say some or all of the following: 'I am a teacher more than a geographer, and a person more than a teacher. I seek to widen the repertoire of techniques I use in the classroom to enable my pupils to grow as persons, talking thoughtfully and respectfully to each other, for I look to their growing commitment to social justice. I hope to extend not only my techniques of teaching but also my skills, so that there is an optimum balance in my classroom of security and challenge. I aspire to deepen my tolerance and my commitment to justice, both in my immediate situation and in the wider world. I seek opportunities for such learning, and moral support, at in-service courses of various kinds. I reckon to improve my political skills, particularly within and around the school where I teach. I recognize that Brian*... speaks for me in some of my moods; but I have other moods also. In these I am a self-managing human being who dares - yes, dares - to be a teacher.'*
>
> *Something like that. At least in a quiet murmur or whisper. Better still, out loud.*"

Richardson, 1983 pages 130-131

* Brian is a disillusioned teacher who declines to be involved in a potentially interesting and worthwhile week-end conference.

Though this passage pre-dates the duties imposed by the National Curriculum, there was nevertheless an irreducible core of obligations in a teacher's work and these, as Robin Richardson makes clear earlier in his Chapter, could sometimes become burdensome and wearing. What is also clear, however, is the sense of the ingredients of the teaching doughnut beyond the core of duties, a sense of personal empowerment, of autonomy, of self-development. And, beyond this, incorporating the whole doughnut and more, the whole person, the whole life.

Bibliography

Adey, P (1991) 'Cognitive acceleration through science education' in Maclure, S and Davies, P (Eds) *Learning to think: thinking to learn,* Oxford, Pergamon/OECD

Adey, P and Shayer, M (1994) *Really Raising Standards: Cognitive intervention and academic achievement* London, Routledge

Bailey, P & Binns, T (1987), *A Case for Geography*, Sheffield, The Geographical Association

Bailey, P and Fox, P (1996) 'Teaching and learning with maps' in Bailey, P and Fox, P (Eds) *Geography Teachers' Handbook,* Sheffield, The Geographical Association

Bailey, P and Fox, P (Eds) (1996) *Geography Teachers' Handbook*, Sheffield, The Geographical Association

Balchin, W G and Coleman, A M (1973) 'Graphicacy should be the fourth ace in the pack in Bale, J, Graves N, and Walford, R (Eds) *Perspectives in Geographical Education,* Edinburgh, Oliver and Boyd

Bale, J (1987) *Geography in the Primary School,* London, Routledge and Kegan Paul

Barrett, H (1996) 'Education without prejudice' in Bailey, P and Fox, P (Eds) *Geography Teachers' Handbook*, Sheffield, The Geographical Association

Battersby, J (1996) *Teaching Geography at Key Stage 3* Cambridge, Chris Kington Publishing

Bennett, N (1993) 'Knowledge bases for learning to teach' in Bennett N and Carré, C (Eds) *Learning to Teach,* London, Routledge

Bennett N and Carré, C (Eds) (1993) *Learning to Teach,* London, Routledge

Bennett, N and Dunne, E (1994) 'How children learn: Implications for practice' in Moon, B and Mayes, A S (Eds) *Teaching and Learning in the Secondary School,* London, Routledge/Open University

Bennetts, T (1986) 'Structure and Progression in Geography' in Boardman, D (Ed.) *Handbook for Geography Teachers,* Sheffield, The Geographical Association

Bennetts, T (1996) 'Progression and differentiation' in Boardman, D (Ed.) *Handbook for Geography Teachers* Sheffield, The Geographical Association

Blyth, A, Cooper, C, Derricott, R, Elliott, G, Sumner, H and Waplington, A (1976) *Place, Time and Society 8 - 13; Curriculum planning in history, geography and social science,* Liverpool, Schools Council Publications

Boardman, D (1983) *Graphicacy and geography teaching* Beckenham, Croom Helm

Boardman, D (1986) (Ed.) *Handbook for Geography Teachers* Sheffield, The Geographical Association

Bresson, F (1991) 'Commentary on Critical Thinking across Multiple Intelligences by Kornhaber and Gardner' in Maclure, S and Davies, P (Eds) *Learning to think: thinking to learn*, Oxford, Pergamon/OECD

Brown, C (1990) 'Personal and Social Education' in Dufour, B (Ed) *The New Social Curriculum,* Cambridge, Cambridge University Press

Brown, G and Wragg, E C (1993) *Questioning,* London, Routledge

Brown, S and McIntyre, D (1993) *Making sense of teaching,* Buckingham, Open University Press

Brown, S (1994) 'Assessment: a changing practice', in Moon, B and Mayes, A S (Eds) *Teaching and Learning in the Secondary School,* London, Routledge/Open University

Bruner, J (1967) *Towards a Theory of Instruction,* Harvard University Press

Bullough, R V, Jr; Knowles, J G and Crow, N A (1991) *Emerging as a Teacher* London; Routledge

Carr, W and Kemmis, S (1986) *Becoming Critical: Education, Knowledge and Action Research*; London, The Falmer Press

Carter, R and Bailey, P (1996) 'Geography in the whole curriculum' in Bailey, P and Fox, P (Eds) *Geography Teachers' Handbook,* Sheffield, The Geographical Association

Chambers, B and Donert, K (1996) *Teaching Geography at Key Stage 2* Cambridge, Chris Kington Publishing

Corney, G (Ed) (1985) *Geography, Schools and Industry,* Sheffield, The Geographical Association

Creemers, B (1994) *The Effective Classroom,* London, Cassell

Curriculum Council for Wales (1991) *Geography in the National Curriculum - Non-Statutory Guidance for Teachers* Cardiff, HMSO

Davidson, G (1996) 'Using OFSTED criteria to develop classroom practice' in *Teaching Geography* Sheffield, Geographical Association

Davis, N (1992) Information Technology in United Kingdom Initial Teacher Education, *The Journal of Information Technology for Teacher Education Vol.1 No.1,* Wallingford UK: Triangle Journals Ltd.

Dean, J (1991) *Professional Development in School*, Milton Keynes, Open University Press

de Bono, E (1991) 'The direct teaching of thinking in education and the CoRT Method' in Maclure, S and Davies, P (Eds) *Learning to think: thinking to learn,* Oxford, Pergamon/OECD

Derricott, R (1994), ' Subjects as Resources: From a Schools Council Project to National Curriculum Geography' in Marsden, B and Hughes, J (Eds), *Primary School Geography,* London, David Fulton Publishers

Department of Education and Science / Welsh Office (1983) *Curriculum 11 - 16: Towards a statement of entitlement* London, HMSO

Department of Education and Science (1986), *Geography for ages 5 - 16: Curriculum matters 7, an HMI series* London, HMSO

Department of Education and Science (1989), *Aspects of Primary Education: The Teaching and Learning of History and Geography* London, HMSO

Department of Education and Science (1990), *Geography for ages 5 - 16: Final Report of the Geography Working Group* London, HMSO

Department For Education (1995), *Geography in the National Curriculum* London, HMSO

Desforges, C (Ed.) (1995) *An Introduction to Teaching: Psychological Perspectives* Oxford, Blackwell

Dockerell, B (1995) 'Approaches to Educational Assessment' in Desforges (Ed.) *An Introduction to Teaching: Psychological Perspectives* Oxford, Blackwell

Dufour, B (Ed) (1990) *The New Social Curriculum,* Cambridge, Cambridge University Press

Elliott, J (1989) 'Teacher Evaluation and Teaching as a Moral Science' in Holly, M and Mcloughlin, C (Eds.) *Perspectives on Teacher Professional Development*, London, Falmer

Fien, J (1983) 'Humanistic Geography' in Huckle, J (Ed.) *Geographical Education: Reflection and Action* Oxford University Press

Fien, J and Gerber, R (Eds) (1988) *Teaching Geography for a Better World,* Edinburgh, Oliver and Boyd

Fisher, T (1996) 'Information Technology and the Curriculum: IT Capability and the New Teacher' in *British Journal of Curriculum and Assessment Vol.6, No.2* London, Hodder and Stoughton

Fox, R (1995) 'Development and Learning' in Desforges (Ed.) *An Introduction to Teaching: Psychological Perspectives* Oxford, Blackwell

Fox, P (1996) 'Where can you go with geography?' in Bailey, P and Fox, P (Eds) *Geography Teachers' Handbook,* Sheffield, The Geographical Association

Geographical Association (1991) *Implementing Geography in the National Curriculum* (leaflets) Sheffield, The Geographical Association

GA/ NCET (1994) *Geography: a pupil's entitlement for IT* Sheffield and Coventry, Geographical Association / National Council for Educational Technology

GA/ NCET (1995[a]) *Primary geography: a pupil's entitlement for IT* Sheffield and Coventry, Geographical Association / National Council for Educational Technology

GA/NCET (1995[b]) *Using IT to enhance geography: case studies at key stages 3 and 4* Sheffield and Coventry, Geographical Association / National Council for Educational Technology

GA/NCET (1995[c]) *Investigating Weather Data - a resource booklet for teachers* Sheffield and Coventry, Geographical Association / National Council for Educational Technology

GA/NCET (1995[d]) *Shopping and Traffic Fieldwork - a resource booklet for teachers* Sheffield and Coventry, Geographical Association / National Council for Educational Technology

Golby, M, Greenwald, J and West, R (1975) *Curriculum Design* London, Croom Helm/Open University Press

Grimwade, K (1996) 'Practical approaches to assessment, record-keeping and reporting' in Bailey, P and Fox, P (Eds) *Geography Teachers' Handbook,* Sheffield, The Geographical Association

Handy, C (1994) *The Empty Raincoat'* London, Arrow

Harris, D and Bell, C (1994) *Evaluating and assessing for learning* London, Kogan Page

Holly, M L (1987) *Keeping a personal professional journal,* Victoria, Australia, Deakin University Press

Holly, M and Mcloughlin, C (Eds.) (1989) *Perspectives on Teacher Professional Development*, London, Falmer

Hicks, D and Holden, C (1995) *Visions of the Future: Why we need to teach for tomorrow* Stoke-on-Trent, Trentham Books

Hillcoat, J (1996), 'Action Research' in Williams, M (Ed) *Understanding Geographical and Environmental Education: The Role of Research* London, Cassell

Hirst, P (1965) 'Liberal education and the nature of knowledge' in Archambault (Ed) *Philosophical Analysis and Education* London, Routledge and Kegan Paul

Hughes, M (1993) *Flexible Learning: Evidence Examined,* Stafford, Network Education Press

Huckle, J (Ed.) (1983) *Geographical Education: Reflection and Action* Oxford University Press

Huckle, J (1991) 'Reasons to be cheerful' in Walford, R (Ed) *Viewpoints on Geography Teaching: The Charney Manor Conference Papers 1990.* Longman

Hughes, J and Marsden, B (1994) 'Resourcing Primary Geography: Bringing the World into the Classroom' in Marsden, B and Hughes, J (Eds), *Primary School Geography,* London, David Fulton Publishers

IUCN, UNEP, WWF (1991) *Caring For the Earth,* IUCN, UNEP, WWF

Kent, A and Phillips, A (1994) 'Geography through Information Technology: Supporting Geographical Enquiry' in Marsden, B and Hughes, J (Eds) *Primary School Geography* London, David Fulton Publishers

Kenyon, J (1994) 'Linking Geography with Mathematics and Science: Curriculum Integration in a Primary School (Enquiry-based Geographical Study' in Marsden, B and Hughes, J (Eds) *Primary School Geography*, London, David Fulton Publishers

Kerry, T and Sands, M (1982) *Handling Classroom groups: a Teaching Skills Workbook,* London, Macmillan Education

Knight, P (1993) *Primary Geography, Primary History* London, David Fulton Publishers

Kompf, M (1995) *'Anticipation and reflection: non-prophet activities?'* Paper presented to the 11th International Congress on Personal Construct Psychology in 1995 at the Ramon Llull University in Barcelona, Spain.

Krause, J (1994) 'Read all about it': Using Children's Literature in Support of Primary Geography in Marsden, B and Hughes, J (Eds), *Primary School Geography,* London, David Fulton Publishers

Kyriacou, C (1991) *Essential Teaching Skills* Cheltenham, Stanley Thornes

Lambert, D (1992) 'Towards a Geography of Social Concern' in Naish, M (Ed) *Geography and Education: National and International Perspectives,* Instutute of Education, University of London.

Lambert, D (1996) 'Issues in assessment' in Bailey, P and Fox, P (Eds) *Geography Teachers' Handbook,* Sheffield, The Geographical Association

Livingstone, D (1992), *The Geographical Tradition: Episodes in the History of a Contested Enterprise*, Oxford, Blackwell.

Maclure, S and Davies, P (Eds) (1991) *Learning to think: thinking to learn - the proceedings of the 1989 OECD Conference organised by the Centre for Educational research and Innovation,* Oxford, Pergamon/OECD

Marsden, B (1994) 'Linking Geography with History and Art: a Focused Topic Work Approach' in Marsden, B and Hughes, J (Eds) *Primary School Geography,* London, David Fulton Publishers

Marsden, B (1995), *Geography 11 - 16: Rekindling Good Practice,* London, David Fulton Publishers

Marsden, B (1994) 'Beyond Locational Knowledge: Good Assessment Practice in Primary Geography' in Marsden, B and Hughes, J (Eds) *Primary School Geography*, London, David Fulton Publishers

Marsden, B and Hughes, J (Eds) (1994), *Primary School Geography*, London, David Fulton Publishers

Mathematical Association (1991) *Develop Your Teaching: A Professional Development Pack for Mathematics - and Other - Teachers,* The Mathematical Association

Martin, F (1996) *Teaching Early Years Geography,* Cambridge, Chris Kington Publishing

Molyneux, F and Tolley, H (1987) *Teaching Geography: A teaching skills workbook* London, Macmillan Education

Moon, B and Mayes, A S (Eds) (1994) *Teaching and Learning in the Secondary School,* London, Routledge/Open University

Morgan, W (1994) 'Making a Place for Geography: The Geographical Association's Initiatives and the Geography Working Group's Experience' in Marsden, B and Hughes, J (Eds) *Primary School Geography,* London, David Fulton Publishers

Morris, J (1992) ' 'Back to the future': the impact of political ideology on the design and implementation of geography in the National Curriculum.' In *The Curriculum Journal* Vol. 3 no. 1

Naish, M (Ed) (1992*) Geography and Education: national and International perspectives*, Instutute of Education, University of London.

National Curriculum Council (1990[a]) *National Curriculum Guidance 3: The Whole Curriculum,* York: The National Curriculum Council

National Curriculum Council (1990[b]) *National Curriculum Guidance 4: Education for Economic and Industrial Understanding,* York: The National Curriculum Council

National Curriculum Council (1990[c]) *National Curriculum Guidance 5: Health Education* York: The National Curriculum Council

National Curriculum Council (1990[d]) *National Curriculum Guidance 6: Careers Education and Guidance,,* York: The National Curriculum Council

National Curriculum Council (1990[e]) *National Curriculum Guidance 7: Environmental Educcation,* York: The National Curriculum Council

National Curriculum Council (1990[f]) *National Curriculum Guidance 8: Education for Citizenship,* York: The National Curriculum Council

National Curriculum Council (1991) *Geography Non-Statutory Guidance York,* York: National Curriculum Council

National Curriculum Council (1992) *Geography and Economic Understanding at Key Stages 3 and 4*, York: National Curriculum Council

NCET (1995) *Approaches to IT capability (leaflets)* Coventry, NCET

NICED (1988) *Guidelines for Primary Schools: Geography* Belfast, NICED / Longman

Nolen, S B (1995) 'Teaching for Autonomous Learning' in Desforges (Ed.) *An Introduction to Teaching: Psychological Perspectives* Oxford, Blackwell

OFSTED (1995) *Geography - A review of inspection findings*, 1993/94 London, HMSO

OFSTED (1996[a]) *Subjects and Standards: Issues for school development arising from OFSTED inspection findings 1994-5, Key Stages 1 & 2,* London, HMSO

OFSTED (1996[b]) *Subjects and Standards: Issues for school development arising from OFSTED inspection findings 1994-5, Key Stages 3 & 4 and Post-16,* London, HMSO

Olson, J (1988) *Schoolworlds / microworlds: computers and the culture of the classroom,* Oxford: Pergamon Press

Palmer, J (1994) *Geography in the early years,* London, Routledge

Paulos., J A (1988) *Innumeracy: Mathematical Illiteracy and its Consequences,* London, Penguin

Pirsig, R M (1976) *Zen and the Art of Motorcycle Maintenance,* London, Corgi/Transworld Publishers Inc.

Postman, N and Weingartner, C (1971) *Teaching as a subversive activity* London, Penguin

Powell, R (1991) *Resources for Flexible Learning* Stafford, Network Education Press

Rainbow, B (1989) *Supported Self Study,* Oxford, Pergamon

Richardson, R (1983) 'Daring to be a teacher' in Huckle, J (Ed.) *Geographical Education: Reflection and Action,* Oxford University Press

Roberts, C (1986) 'Patriarchy, ethnocentrism and integration' in Holly, D (Ed) *Humanism in adversity*, London, Falmer

Rogers, C (1983) *Freedom to Learn for the 80's,* London, Merrill

Runnymede Trust (1993) *Equality Assurance in Schools: Quality, Identity Society - a handbook for action planning and school effectiveness* Stoke-on-Trent, Trentham Books with The Runnymede Trust

SCAA (1994) *Geography in the National Curriculum: Draft Proposals* London, SCAA

SCAA (1996[a]) *Consistency in Teacher Assessment - Exemplification of Standards, Geography: Key Stage 3* London, SCAA

SCAA (1996[b]) *Teaching Environmental Matters Through the National Curriculum* London, SCAA

SCAA / ACAC (1996) *A guide to the National Curriculum* London, SCAA

Schön, D (1987) *Educating the Reflective Practitioner*, San Francisco, Josey Bass

Sebba, J (1995) *Geography for All* London, David Fulton Publishers

Shah, I (1968) *The Way of the Sufi* London, Penguin

Slater, F (1982), *Learning Through Geography*, London, Heinemann Educational Books

Slater, F (Ed) (1989) *Language and Learning in the Teaching of Geography* London, Routledge

Steiner, M (1996) Evaluating Global Education in Williams, M (Ed) *Understanding Geographical and Environmental Education: The Role of Research* London, Cassell

Stern, J (1995) *Learning to Teach: a guide for school-based initial and in-service training* London, David Fulton Publishers

Stones, E (1992) *Quality Teaching: a sample of cases,* London, Routledge

Thacker, J (1995) 'Personal, Social and Moral Education' in Desforges, C (Ed*.) An Introduction to Teaching: Psychological Perspectives* Oxford, Blackwell

Tolley, H, Biddulph, M and Fisher, T (1996) *Beginning Teaching Workbooks 1 to 6* Cambridge, Chris Kington Publishing

Townsend, S (1984) *The Secret Diary of Adrian Mole aged 13³/₄*, Basingstoke, M Books/Macmillan Educational

TTA (1997) *Standards for the Award of Qualified Teacher Status,* London, TTA

University of Newcastle School of Education (1995) *Improving students' Performance: A guide to thinking skills in education and training* Newcastle-upon-Tyne, Tyneside TEC

Usher, R and Edwards, R (1994) *Postmodernism and Education: Different voices, Different Worlds,* London, Routletge

Walford, R (Ed) (1985) *Geographical Education for a Multi-Cultural Society* Sheffield, The Geographical Association

Walford, R (Ed.) (1991) *Viewpoints on Geography Teaching: The Charney Manor Conference Papers 1990.* Longman

Walford, R and Haggett, P (1995) 'Geography and Geographical education: Some speculations for the twenty-first century' in *Geography,* 80, pages 3 - 13

Waterhouse, K (1991) *Flexible Learning,* Stafford, Network Education Press

Waterhouse, K (1991) *Tutoring,* Stafford, Network Education Press

Wiegand, P (1992) *Places in the Primary School: Knowledge and Understanding of Places at Key Stages 1 and 2,* London, Falmer

Williams, M (Ed) (1981) *Language Teaching and Learning 2: Geography,* London, Ward Lock Educational

Williams, M (Ed) (1996) *Understanding Geographical and Environmental Education: The Role of Research,* London, Cassell

Wynne, T E (1973) 'Geography and the curriculum' in Bale, J, Graves N, and Walford, R (Eds) *Perspectives in Geographical Education* Edinburgh, Oliver and Boyd

Index